MILITARY
AIRCRAFT
TODAY

Soviet Mi-24 (HIND-E) attack helicopter

SEPECAT Jaguar at low level (*photograph courtesy British Aerospace*)

MILITARY AIRCRAFT TODAY

Chris McAllister

ARCO PUBLISHING, INC.
New York

By the same author

Aircraft Alive
aviation and air traffic for enthusiasts (1980)

Planes and Airports (1981)

Jet Liners (1982)

Published by Arco Publishing, Inc.
215 Park Avenue South, New York, NY 10003

© Chris McAllister 1985
First published 1985

Library of Congress Cataloging in Publication Data

McAllister, Chris,
  Military aircraft today.

  Includes index.
  1. Airplanes, Military. I. Title.
UG1240.M39 1985   358.4   84-28373
ISBN 0-668-06503-6 (pbk)

Printed in Great Britain

Contents

Acknowledgment

I am indebted to all those persons and organizations who supplied me with help, information, photographs and research facilities. In the course of these researches I was privileged to meet many people – too many, unfortunately to mention by name – who, in their different and individual ways, made very valuable contributions to my work on this book. However I *can* publicly thank the Royal Air Force, the Royal Navy, British Aerospace, Westland Helicopters, McDonnell-Douglas, Lockheed, Shorts, Northrop, General Dynamics, Fokker, Grumman, Bell Helicopters, Hughes Helicopters, Rolls-Royce Limited, Ferranti, Thomson-CSF, Avions Marcel Dassault-Breguet Aviation, Marconi Avionics Limited, Hollandse Signaalapparaten, The Fleet Air Arm Museum, Royal Netherlands Air Force, Force Aerienne Belge, Royal Danish Air Force, the Austrian Bundesministerium für Landesverteidigung, US Army, US Navy, US Air Force (Europe), NATO, US Mission to NATO, SHAPE, TASS, Central Office of Information, Flight International and Air Pictorial. I would also like to thank Ray Meakin, John Downey, Ralph Watson and Val Caldwell for their practical help, and my wife Ann and daughters, Jo and Sarah, for their continuing help, encouragement and support.

Chris McAllister
January 1984

Foreword

Most aviation enthusiasts tend to swear allegiance to one or other of the two main (and sometimes rival) followings – and, having written three books on the former, – *Aircraft Alive* (B.T. Batsford Ltd, 1980), *Planes and Airports* (B.T. Batsford Ltd), and *Jet Liners* (B.T. Batsford Ltd), – I decided to adapt the approach which had proved successful in these to the rather more difficult theme of present-day military aircraft. This would mean writing a book which would be somewhat different in style and layout from most of those which inhabit the military aviation shelves of libraries and bookshops; whether they be descriptions of a single aircraft type, slices of recent or not-so-recent military aviation history, or encyclopaedic catalogues of every known type of warplane, densely packed with facts and figures. What seemed to be lacking was a book which *explains* military aircraft, not only the planes and engines, but the weapons systems and avionics, and the training and tactics behind the tasks which they may be called upon to perform.

As with the other books, I would hope to develop and deepen the reader's interest in and involvement with military aviation. I hope I can lead him (or her) beyond a sterile preoccupation with 'reggies' – the letters and numbers of registration codes – towards a more rewarding understanding of what air power is all about. Mike Jerram, writing for *Pilot* magazine, tells this story;

> . . . Well, quite frankly there *is* something schoolboyish about a 50-year-old who has never graduated beyond the telescope and notebook stage, growth stunted by a bland diet of alphabet soup registration letters. I met one recently whose foreknowledge of American military aircraft deployments around Europe would have stripped the threads of the Kremlin's thumbscrews. 'Course,' he confided, 'I don't know anything *about* the planes. It's just the numbers painted on them that interest me.'

It is true that military aircraft are far less accessible than their civilian counterparts. Visitors are welcome (or at least tolerated) at civil airports. They can watch airliners and business aircraft at close range or listen in to the ATC chatter on pocket radios. On the other hand, it is not possible to tune in easily, if at all, to military radios, and military airfields are only open to the public on certain selected days each year. Nevertheless, for the dedicated military aviation enthusiast, there are compensations. Perhaps it is because warplanes are inherently more interesting: They have a greater variety of tasks to perform, – whether it be air defence, ground attack, reconnaissance, flight refuelling or humble trucking with supplies – and a number of interesting ways of going about these jobs. There is also a much wider range of types of military aircraft. After a couple of days spent at a major civil airport, particularly during the summer months, you will have seen 95 per cent of what the world of civil aviation has to offer. Not so with military aircraft: there is always something new to seek out and photograph; something new to discover, some new revelation, some new insight into the design of the aircraft, their systems or tactics.

To the layman, the world of military aviation may appear closed, secretive, well defended and to some extent sinister in its preoccupation with technological violence or the threat of Armageddon. To the initiated, however, be they aviation enthusiasts or armchair strategists, it can be a fascinating intellectual challenge to try to gain some understanding of today's military aviation scene. It is also very necessary, in a democratic society, to be able to check out some of the incompetence which may

hide beneath the cloak of official secrecy, supposedly in the national interest. However, as far as official secrecy is concerned, I can offer no help. All I can do is to assist readers to begin to understand what some aircraft and systems are designed to do and of what they are potentially capable. I can provide a map to help readers pick their way through the minefield of technological jargon, acronyms and 'yuckspeak'. Acronyms are explained in the text as they occur, and there is a combined Index and Glossary at the end of the book.

A book such as this can serve only as an introduction. It will, I hope, leave the reader slightly better prepared to pursue his interest through other channels such as flying displays, more books, the news media and authoritative publications such as *Flight International*. Certainly the best way is to join a club. There are well-established and well-run aviation societies in most parts of Britain, and a phone call to the public relations office at the local airfield or airport will help you locate those near you. These clubs and aviation societies organize regular meetings, trips to exhibitions and flying displays, etc. Many have clubrooms and newsletters; others specialise in getting their hands dirty restoring old aeroplanes.

1 The Panavia Tornado F.2 long-range fighter will form the backbone of Britain's air-defence squadrons from about 1985 onwards, supplementing ageing Lightnings and Phantoms now in service. The F.2 is a version of the multi- national, multi-role swing-wing Tornado, the most important military aircraft to have been built in Western Europe since World War II. (*British Aerospace*)

1 Air Power Today

Military aircraft are a necessary evil. We do not live in a perfect world and, for as long as human nature remains basically unchanged, there will always be people and nations who will want to use military force to take advantage of their fellow men. Unfortunately, this is no less true today when the means of waging war have become more sophisticated and destructively powerful than ever before. Peace has to be founded upon deterrence; the same capabilities and technology, including military aircraft, that would be used for aggression are also the best defence against aggression. Deterrence, though a paradox, does work. The primary purpose of a Tornado or a Mirage is to wage war but, by showing that they can do so effectively, they are more likely to prevent a war than to start one. The price we pay for peace founded upon deterrence, however, is an arms race where each 'side' tries to outscore a potential enemy by upgrading and modernizing its military capability and technology, including aircraft.

It is the rivalry between the two Superpowers and their respective allies which provides the chief impetus for the continuing development of military aircraft. Yesterday's jets are not only old and difficult to maintain, but they are likely to be outclassed by the newer, more expensive and more complex machines and weapons systems being designed and built at present. Some of the high costs of developing new aircraft can be offset by export sales and there is a thriving market among so-called 'non-aligned' countries for military aircraft of all types to fill almost every conceivable role.

It is easy to understand why a small country in some remote corner of the globe might want to buy, or even build, some kinds of military aircraft. Those with offshore waters need some means of patrolling them; a general-purpose aircraft fitted with a suitable radar, or even a helicopter can do the job better than a patrol boat. Helicopters and transport aircraft can earn a living by airlifting government officials and VIPs in areas where roads are bad or almost non-existent. And, if bigger loads need to be carried, there will always be work for something the size of the Lockheed C-130 Hercules. Over 1700 'Herks' have been built, and they are operated by the air forces of 55 nations, making the Hercules what is surely the most widely distributed and possibly the most familiar military aircraft in the world. Apart from its chief task of airlifting (or dropping) troops, equipment, vehicles or supplies, the Hercules can transform itself into an Angel of Mercy should disaster strike, bringing relief to victims or evacuating those in need of medical care.

But the world-wide growth of air power doesn't stop with the sale of tactical transports such as the 'Herk.' Aircraft with an offensive capability, such as fighters, are also being sold in large numbers to most of the world's nations, who feel that they need modern airpower for dealing with (or threatening to deal with) their internal and external enemies, real or potential. The French have successfully sold their Mirage range of fighters to nearly 30 countries, often in the face of stiff competition from the US, Britain, and even the Soviet Union, all of whom have scored notable sales successes themselves. The US has built over 5000 McDonnell-Douglas Phantom IIs since 1958. Designed originally as an air-defence fighter for the US Navy, the powerful Phantom became the most versatile jet fighter of all time, turning its hand to reconnaissance, ground attack and close support as well as air defence, meanwhile serving with the air forces of 12 nations, including Britain, West Germany, Greece and Turkey, most of whom still rely on the Phantom as a front-line aircraft.

2 The Boeing B-52 Stratofortress originally entered service 30 years ago designed for high-altitude strategic bombing with free-fall nuclear bombs. Since then, these BUFFs (Big Ugly Fat Fellas) have been upgraded and modified many times, and adapted to a variety of different roles, including missile launching. The version shown here is the turbofan re-engined B-52H, which has a combat radius of more than 4000 miles (6400km), and in this case is armed with 12 AGM-69A SRAMs (Short Range Attack Missiles). (*Photograph courtesy Boeing*)

Britain has sold Hunters world-wide and Lightnings in the Middle East. Hawks are still being sold widely, including a navalized version to the US Navy. Sea Harriers are being sold to India, and a version of the design is being produced for the US Marine Corps. Jaguars are exported to Oman and Nigeria. The Soviet Union is competing in the same market, anxious to earn foreign currency or political influence or both, by equipping the air forces of its client states with export versions of the latest MiGs and Sukhois.

Sales of aircraft go hand in hand with sales of spares and equipment, including: weapons, guns, ammunition, bombs, rockets, missiles, napalm and the whole destructive panoply of modern aerial fire-power. Sadly, the sale of aircraft and weapons to countries that can ill afford them is big business. Many people argue that it is a bad business; that the arms trade, like the arms race, can end only in disaster. The moral, political and even religious arguments which rage around these two topics are well known, if little understood. They are certainly very complex and well beyond the scope of this book.

Plenty of other complex issues remain, however. A military aircraft begs a question which hopefully will never be asked; can it do its job? Only a war can provide a clear answer and, despite all the operational testing, all the computer-simulated war games and peacetime exercises, no war is ever a carbon copy of one that went before. The next war is an adventure in uncertainty which should almost at all costs be avoided. However, it would only be afterwards that the aviation historians would be able to answer the question as to whether a particular aeroplane, weapons system, tactical or training philosophy was able to do the job for which it was designed. The paradox of deterrence is that war can be prevented only by planning to fight unfought wars. The planning has to be ongoing and continuous, and one of the spin-offs from this idea as far as a particular military aeroplane is concerned is that its role and purpose may change many times during its service lifetime.

CHANGING ROLES

Where, for example, have all the bombers gone? Thirty years ago they were very much around: Boeing B-52 Stratofortress, Canberra, Victor, Vulcan, Myasishchev M-4 (*Bison*), Tu-95 (*Bear*). Designed to fly high, where the air is thin and fuel consumption is more favourable and to drop free-fall nuclear or conventional bombs on distant targets, they were in the front line of the world's large air forces, ready at a moment's notice to carry the war to an enemy. Then it was that anti-bomber defences improved: sophisticated air-defence radars and high-flying missiles made it difficult for these big bombers to get through unless they changed their tactics. They could no longer risk a high-altitude run-in to their targets because they would show too easily on radar. It now became necessary to develop low-flying techniques to outwit enemy defences, taking advantage of such natural features as hills in order to remain hidden from the all-seeing eyes of the radars. But the big bombers of the 'fifties are ungainly performers at low-level and their combat radius is considerably shortened by having to operate in the dense air near the ground. Low-level strikes are probably best carried out by fighter-type aircraft rather than those originally designed mainly for high-altitude bombing.

The big bombers are still around, converted now to somewhat different roles. The RAF's Canberras are used mainly for photo-reconnaissance and electronic warfare, while the Victors have been earning their living for years as flight-refuelling tankers. The Vulcan soldiered on, pretending it was a low-level strike weapon, until finally, just before it was due to retire in 1982, a chance came for it to drop bombs in anger on Stanley airfield during the longest bombing raids in history, air-to-air refuelled by Victors from and back to Ascension Island. As a consequence of this eve-of-retirement success, the Vulcans have not all been pensioned off to aviation museums or as gate guardians. Some are still in service as tankers.

During its equally long career, the USAF's Boeing B-52 has undergone a number of modifications and role changes. There are still more than 300 B-52s in USAF service as conventional bombers, missile launchers, electronic warfare platforms and the like. Meanwhile the Russians' mighty Tupolev Tu-95 (*Bear*), once a long-range strategic bomber, is enjoying a completely new lease of life in the electronic warfare, maritime-reconnaissance and anti-submarine roles, so much so that the production line has been started up again after a shutdown of many years, and the type has been re-designated Tu-142. It is still on record in an age of jets as being the fastest operational propeller-driven aircraft and the only one with swept wings, capable of a speed of over 500mph at altitude.

At a public military air display or at a 'shop window' event such as Farnborough or the Paris Salon, it is difficult to find a genuine bomber any more. Instead there are fighters, fighter-bombers, interdiction-strike aircraft, ground-attack aircraft and so on, all of them embodying the schoolboy's stereotype of the jet fighter: swept wings, sharply pointed nose and a variety of cigar-shaped appendages dangling from the wings. The wing pylons all have standard attachments: remove a long-range fuel tank and hook on a bomb instead. There are big bombs and little bombs, gun packs, rocket packs, Sidewinder or Matra missiles for air-to-air combat, anti-armour bombs, anti-runway bombs, air-to-surface missiles, reconnaissance pods, electronic warfare pods, and so on. Choose your weapons. The old and easy distinction between fighters and bombers is no longer clear. It all depends on what you hang under the wings, and instead of 'fighter' and 'bomber' we have terms such as 'tactical aircraft', 'fast jet' or 'multi-role combat aircraft', which try to describe more accurately what front-line military aircraft are all about.

More than any other single factor, it is the development of ground-based air-defence radars which has forced the bombers to come down out of the stratosphere and has brought about today's generation of tactical aircraft equipped for the new low-level role of high-speed, below-the-radar attack. By a more-or-less happy coincidence, the kind of supersonic, rugged airframe, designed originally for high-altitude interception, also turned out to be suitable for low-level strike. High-powered engines for acceleration, high-lift wings capable either of tight turns in air combat or, alternatively, of lifting heavy bombs and extra fuel tanks from a short runway, swept-back wings and a rugged structure for dashing through transonic turbulence at low-level are all features of today's tactical aircraft, whether its main role is ground attack or air-to-air combat.

The Tornado

The multi-national Tornado is, without doubt, the most important tactical aeroplane to have been produced in Europe so far. Despite its earlier title of 'multi-role combat aircraft', there are indeed two versions of the swing-wing

3 Another big bomber of the 'fifties, the Soviet Tupolev Tu-95, codenamed *Bear* by NATO, is enjoying a new lease of life in various roles. Shown here is a *Bear-C* of Soviet Naval Aviation, used for maritime reconnaissance.

4 A typical scene from the static park at Farnborough 1982 shows a Jaguar armed with Matra Magic air-to-air missiles, BL755 cluster bombs and long-range fuel tanks, surrounded by other types of lethal hardware, such as the Harpoon anti-ship missile, the Matra Durandal concrete-piercing bomb, rocket pods and a mock-up of the British Aerospace ALARM anti-radar missile.

Tornado, the Interdiction Strike version (IDS) and the Air Defence version (ADV). In some ways the Tornado can be compared to the General Dynamics F-111 strike aircraft or the Sukhoi Su-24 (*Fencer*). Like the Tornado, both of these have swing wings and are designed to fly at low level in all weathers, hidden from enemy radars. The Tornado is the most recent design of the three, powered by newly designed, fuel-efficient RB.199 turbofans and the latest avionics, radar and weapons systems. The Tornado is being produced in quantity for the Royal Air Force, the West German Luftwaffe and Marineflieger, plus the Aeronautica Militare Italiano. It can be relied upon to penetrate enemy air space day or night in all weathers, flying at tree-top height faster than any other aircraft and, in a very hostile electronic environment, find and destroy its target, using a variety of accurately positioned conventional weapons, and then get home again.

The Tornado ADV, which is being developed solely for the RAF, will have the demanding role of defending UK airspace (which stretches from Iceland to the Baltic) against massive numbers of attackers, should the need ever arise. The Tornado ADV, or Tornado F.2 as it will be known in RAF service, can patrol far out over the Atlantic or the North Sea for over four hours without refuelling, armed with Sky Flash advanced, medium-range, air-to-air missiles. Instead of mixing it with the opposition in tail-chasing dogfights, the Tornado F.2's weapons systems are designed to enable it to identify hostile aircraft at long range and to attack these head-on with radar-guided Sky Flash missiles while they are still anything up to 30 miles (50km) away.

The Tornado is, however, an expensive aeroplane, the cost of each one being reckoned at some £15 million. Like Concorde, another expensive but important machine, the Tornado has been the subject of much criticism in the press, the main target of the criticism being the cost to the taxpayer. It has been suggested that the Tornado programme is too ambitious: that the swing wing is an unnecessary and expensive complication, that there was no need to have developed a brand-new engine, that most of the Tornado's sophisticated electronic gadgetry is unnecessary, and that the same job could be done better either by missiles or by larger numbers of smaller, simpler (and consequently cheaper) fighters. I doubt it. If there is to be another war in Europe, it is not likely to start in broad daylight in clear weather, but more probably in winter, during rain, fog or snow. The opposition might very well consist of thousands of the latest Soviet all-weather tactical aircraft. It will need a weapons system of exceptional quality to face this kind of opposition should the situation arise. And, if it ever does, one of the things we shall be defending will be the right to disagree about whether or not we need Tornadoes at all.

Missiles or Manned Aircraft

The argument about using missiles rather than manned aircraft has been rumbling on for nearly 30 years. A missile is much cheaper than a manned aircraft and is designed to be expendable. A surface-to-air missile can be used for air defence, but not under all circumstances. Unlike a Tornado F.2, it cannot be used to provide defence-in-depth over very long ranges, and again, unlike a Tornado, it cannot just go up and take a look if one is unsure of what the threat is or whether, indeed, there is a threat at all. A surface-to-surface missile begins to look like an attractive alternative to the IDS Tornado for penetrating well-defended, hostile airspace. Could one design a missile big enough and clever enough to destroy difficult targets such as airfields or advancing armoured columns, and to outwit enemy defences, including sophisticated jamming systems, while doing so? Perhaps not yet. Even the 'smartest' missiles are still fairly 'dumb' and are difficult to reprogramme to respond to changes in defence tactics. Neither can they carry large conventional warheads. The manned interdictor aircraft, such as the Tornado with its highly-trained crew, may be much more expensive and less expendable than a missile, and will be taking a proportionately much greater risk but, even in the midst of today's advanced and deadly military technology, it is a more flexible and adaptable weapons system and, as such, more likely to get through.

The Multi-role Philosophy

One answer to the high cost of developing new aircraft types has been the multi-role philosophy: one design capable of performing many different roles, e.g. air defence, ground attack, reconnaissance, electronic warfare. Tornado is a good example, as are the new Mirage 2000 and Mirage 4000 or the McDonnell-Douglas/Northrop F/A-18 Hornet. The Hornet was developed as a combined fighter (F) and attack (A) aircraft for the US Navy and Marines, hence the unusual prefix F/A. The Hornet was not to have the complication of a swing wing, but, instead, an advanced fixed wing was developed, while structure weight was saved by large-scale use of plastic composites instead of metal. Advanced cockpit displays were used to make the single pilot's task easier, aided by what is widely regarded as one of the best multimode radars in the business, the Hughes APG-65. The Hornet is being sold abroad to Canada, Spain and Australia.

THE TACTICAL USES OF AIR POWER

The low-level strike philosophy built into modern combat aircraft, such as the Tornado IDS and its weapons systems, is an integral part of present-day thinking about the tactical uses of air power. Air power is crucial to success in any land or sea battle, and it is an essential military objective to establish air supremacy over the battle zone from Day One.

The favoured method of doing this will be to employ what are called *counter-air* tactics: i.e., to launch carefully timed surprise attacks against the enemy's airfields.

Coming in low below the radar, attacking aircraft would hope to catch the defending aircraft on the ground before they have a chance to take off, and to put the airfield out of action or to render it unusable for at least 24 hours. Specially designed concrete-piercing bombs would try to crater and fracture the runways and destroy any aircraft hiding inside concrete Hardened Aircraft Shelters (HAS), and chemical weapons containing nerve gases would either kill most of the personnel on the base or make it very difficult for them to repair the damage quickly while having to wear pro-

5 The McDonnell-Douglas/Northrop F/A-18 Hornet multi-role combat aircraft undergoing carrier-landing trials. (*Photograph courtesy McDonnell-Douglas*)

tective NBC (Nuclear Biological Chemical) clothing.

It is no secret that this is how the air forces of the Warsaw Pact are intending to fight should a war ever break out in Europe. Fighter-bombers such as the MiG-23 and MiG-27 have been developed specially for the counter-air role: able to fly fast and low in all weathers and to deliver bombs where they will do most damage with precise accuracy. If the Warsaw Pact forces could mount a successful surprise attack, most NATO airfields in West Germany, Denmark, Holland and Belgium, and also those in France and south-eastern Britain would be at risk.

The best defence against this form of surprise attack is to remove the element of surprise. Terrain-hugging, low-flying attackers may be invisible to many ground-based radars but not to airborne radars carried by Airborne Early Warning (AEW) aircraft such as the RAF's Nimrod AEW.3 and the Boeing E-3 AWACS (Airborne Warning and Command Station). In effect, these aircraft are flying radar stations with the ability to 'look down' and pick out low-flying aircraft against the cluttered background

6 The major threat to European airfields may come from the MiG-23 swing-wing all-weather counter-air fighter, designed to attack opposing air forces while they are still on the ground.

7 A prototype of the Interdictor Strike version of the Tornado takes off from its Warton, Lancashire base carrying eight 1000lb (454kg) bombs, long-range fuel tanks and Marconi Skyshadow electronic warfare self-protection jamming pods. (*Photograph courtesy British Aerospace*)

8 The McDonnell-Douglas F-4 Phantom II was widely regarded in the 1960s as the best fighter in the world, and many are still in front-line service with a number of air forces, including the RAF. Shown here is a Phantom F-4E of the Turkish Air Force. (*Photograph courtesy McDonnell-Douglas*)

of radar echoes being returned from the landscape. The range of these airborne radars is over 200 miles (300km), and they would provide several minutes warning of any 'surprise' attack. This would allow the defenders sufficient time to get their own air forces into the air and to alert their missile defences. While the attackers were trying to neutralize the defenders' airfields, the defenders themselves would be carrying out a counter-attack, hoping to neutralize the attackers' airfields, thereby leaving them nowhere to land and refuel on their return. This too, would be a 'counter-air' operation and, in NATO's case, would rely heavily on F-111s, Tornadoes, Jaguars, Phantoms, F-5s and Buccaneers.

The real difficulty is that it is not possible at the present time to re-equip an air force overnight with the very latest aircraft and weapon systems. The cost would be far too high, and even NATO's front line has to rely on aircraft which are getting a bit long in the tooth. The most widely deployed tactical aircraft in NATO is the McDonnell-Douglas F-4 Phantom, which equips units of the USAF in Britain and Germany, the West German Luftwaffe, the Spanish, Greek and Turkish air forces, plus the RAF. The roles for which these Phantoms are equipped vary from air defence (RAF) to ground attack, reconnaissance, electronic warfare and defence suppression. But whereas the Phantom was the miracle

fighter of the sixties, it would probably be at a disadvantage in the more difficult air-combat environments of the eighties.

Air Defence

In the US Navy, the Phantom has been replaced by the Grumman F-14 Tomcat, and in the US Air Force by the McDonnell-Douglas F-15 Eagle. Both of these new fighters are said to be fast enough to catch Russia's Mach 3 plus MiG-25 Foxbat on a good day. Other European air forces are also re-equipping with new fighters, Holland, Belgium, Norway and Denmark have chosen the General Dynamics F-16 Fighting Falcon which is being built under licence by Fokker at Schiphol and by the Belgian company SABCA/SONACA at Gosselies.

The tactical thinking which lies behind the choice of the powerful F-15 Eagle and the smaller F-16 Falcon to provide the air defence of NATO's vital Central Region in Europe is that the potential enemy threat is only a few minutes flying time from NATO air bases. These are 'air-superiority' fighters, designed to be more than a match for any potential opponent on a one-to-one or even several-to-one basis, especially at close range. Power, agility and good weapons systems are the ingredients of air superiority under Central Region conditions.

The air defence of the United Kingdom in time of war rests upon a different tactical concept from that of Central Europe. Britain's island status confers on it several advantages. There would be plenty of warning of an attack being launched across the Low Countries, the Baltic, or the North Sea, Attacking aircraft flying low

9 Armourers wearing NBC protective clothing re-arm an RAF Phantom for its major role as an air-defence interceptor. Sidewinder and Sky Flash missiles are fitted, plus long-range fuel tanks and a seven-barrel SUU-20 rotary cannon on the centreline pylon. (*Photograph courtesy RAF*)

over the sea would show up clearly on AEW radar and they would have to penetrate several defensive cordons to reach their targets.

The first line of defence is provided by RAF Strike Command's Phantoms armed with Sky Flash medium-range radar-homing missiles, Sidewinder heat-seeking missiles and cannon. From 1985 onwards the Tornado ADV will enter service with the RAF. This will have improved radar, improved missiles and a much longer Combat Air Patrol (CAP) endurance than that of the Phantom. Anything which manages to get through the defensive screens posed by Tornadoes and Phantoms will still have to run the gauntlet of BAC Lightning short-range interceptors of the 'sixties vintage, Hawks armed with

Sidewinders, and Bloodhound and Rapier missile batteries.

Ground Attack

Ground attack is the other side of the coin from air defence, and this can mean anything from Counter-Insurgency (CoIn) operations against rebels at one end of the scale to the more demanding roles, such as deep penetration attacks (Interdiction), nuclear strike or battlefield close support.

Counter Insurgency

Many types of aircraft, including light planes, are capable of being armed with guns, bombs, rockets and missiles for the least demanding of these tasks. The Argentine-built Pucara is a good example of a cheap, purpose-designed CoIn aircraft. Other planes, designed mainly as trainers, can be 'beefed-up' to carry weapons,

10 The one the others aim to catch. Russia's MiG-25 (NATO reporting name Foxbat) is reputed to be the world's fastest fighter, capable of short bursts at more than three times the speed of sound.

and are cheap to buy and operate: for example the British Aerospace Hawk and Strikemaster, the Cessna A-37, and many more. These aircraft have no radars and can operate only in daylight, but it is unlikely that they will have to contend with anything more troublesome than small arms fire from the ground.

Interdiction Strike Aircraft

The really difficult ground attack roles are those which call for deep penetration of enemy territory, particularly at night or in bad weather. Sophisticated enemy defences, especially radars, are a problem, and it is necessary to foil these by flying very low, taking full advantage of hills and valleys, to outwit them by jamming, or to destroy them with anti-radar missiles. Meanwhile, missiles launched at the attacking aircraft must be decoyed away by dropping 'chaff' and flares. All of this means that the attacking aircraft must be extremely capable and well-equipped.

For example, the IDS version of the Tornado can carry, in addition to its normal warload of bombs or air-to-surface missiles, long-range fuel tanks, electronic warfare or electronic counter-measure (ECM) pods, chaff and flare dispensers, and anti-radar missiles. To enable it to reach its target by a suitably devious route, each Tornado has a high-quality, ground-mapping radar, coupled with an accurate inertial navigation system. To enable the bombs to hit a point target no bigger than a tennis-court in conditions of darkness, low cloud, rain or strong winds, the radar and navigation systems

are in turn linked to a weapons-aiming computer, which not only holds the Tornado on the correct course during its bombing runs, but also selects the precise split-second at which to release the bombs.

IDS aircraft comparable to Europe's Tornado are the USAF's F-111, the US Navy's A-6 Intruder and the Soviet Su-24 Fencer. A larger aircraft with similar but longer-range capability is the US Air force's Rockwell B-1B.

Towards a Flying Tank

Whatever happens in the air, war is about territory on the ground being fought for and won. Modern armies rely heavily on tanks to enable them to move forward quickly on the ground, and air power is seen as a feasible form of defence against large tank formations, or in providing *close support* over the land battlefield. When it comes to bombing tanks from the air, destroying columns of motorised vehicles, or dealing with enemy emplacements and vital structures such as bridges and command centres, three special ingredients are necessary: communication, accuracy and timing.

The pilot of a close-support aircraft must have a radio link which will allow him to talk directly to the field commanders during the course of a battle. Then, if a target is found which can best be dealt with by means of an air strike, say an accurately placed 1000lb (450kg) bomb, the field commander can call up an air strike quickly. Accuracy is the second requirement.

The RAF in Germany have a number of squadrons of SEPECAT Jaguars and Harriers dedicated to the battlefield close-support role. Both these aircraft have a laser-ranging gunsight which enables bombs and other weapons to be released accurately; either the pilot identifies the target first by eye, or the field commander tells the aircraft's weapon-aiming computer (via the pilot) exactly where the target is. Laser-designators can also be used to

11 Even the turn of speed of the MiG-25 is not enough to outrun any of the six long-range Phoenix missiles carried by the US Navy's Grumman F-14 Tomcat. (*Photograph courtesy Grumman*)

12 and 13 Much of the responsibility for maintaining NATO air supremacy in western Europe rests with these new fighters.

12 General Dynamics F-16 Fighting Falcons of the Belgian Air Force. (*Photograph courtesy Force Aerienne Belge*)
13 McDonnell-Douglas F-15 Eagles of the USAF, based at Soesterberg, Holland. (*Photograph courtesy McDonnell-Douglas*)

14 The FMA Pucara was developed in Argentina specifically for light ground-attack and counter-insurgency duties armed with two cannon and four machine guns. This example on display in Britain in 1982 was captured almost intact on East Falkland.

15 A Fairchild Republic A-10 Thunderbolt II of the US Air Force formates on the wingtip of a KC-135 flight-refuelling tanker. (*Photograph courtesy John Downey*)

mark the target, but this system works best only in clear weather.

The Harrier does have an important virtue in that it is independent of airfields, and 'Harrier Hides' are easy to construct in, for example, the corner of a forest. An RAF Harrier GR3 can sit around in its hide until called upon by a field commander; other close-support aircraft have to take off and loiter somewhere just off-stage, burning up precious fuel.

The nearest to a flying tank is perhaps the Republic Fairchild A-10 Thunderbolt II: a rugged aeroplane which can take a lot of punishment from ground fire. The pilot sits in what is virtually an armoured bathtub surrounded by several tons of bombs or missiles, plus a huge, seven-barrel, rotary cannon capable of delivering 70 rounds of 30mm cannon shells per second.

Battlefield Helicopters

Helicopters have a number of advantages when providing close support during a land battle. Like the Harrier, they can be deployed suitably

16 Although it would win no prizes in a beauty contest, the Hughes AH-64 Apache advanced attack helicopter would bring a new dimension of lethality to any battlefield. The Apache is armed with a machine-gun, 38 folding-fin unguided rockets, 16 Hellfire laser-guided anti-tank missiles and equipped with a range of all-weather sensors and aiming systems. (*Photograph courtesy Hughes*)

close at hand, waiting for the most effective moment to move in and strike. A helicopter can fly 'nap of the earth' remaining concealed behind low hills and belts of trees and scrub, popping up only to fire missiles with shaped-charge warheads at targets such as tanks. The helicopter gunship came of age in Vietnam, and the Americans' Bell AH-1 Cobra assault helicopter has now been joined by the AH-64 Apache, the British Army's Lynx and the Russian Mi-8 and Mi-24. Most of these are ugly machines, menacing and deadly, but if one of them appears from behind a hill intent upon killing you, you probably won't be too bothered about its looks anyway! In a land battle helicopters have a number of other useful capabilities, provided they are large enough and well enough equipped. They can ferry troops and evacuate casualties, and they are also good at penetrating behind enemy lines, landing commandos to destroy bridges and other vital targets. The Mil Mi-24 Hind assault helicopter has accommodation for up to eight fully armed troops in addition to its normal complement of guns and anti-tank missiles.

ELECTRONIC WARFARE

Electronic warfare is a mystery to most laymen who tend to think of military aircraft in terms of fast jets armed with guns, bombs and missiles. But a single, humble, lumbering transport aircraft, possibly a converted airliner, carrying a large generator and powerful transmitters, can assume a tactical importance far greater than the latest strike fighter. It can do this by 'noise jamming' on a broad range of frequencies, rendering useless almost all the military radios and radars over a wide area and making the vital tactical functions of *Command, Control, Communication and Intelligence* (C^3I) almost impossible.

Active noise jamming is, however, one of the simplest and crudest kinds of Electronic Countermeasures (ECM) and cannot always be relied upon to be totally effective. There are ways of beating the jammers (known as ECCM – Electronic Counter Countermeasures). Designers of radio and radar systems must try to stay one step ahead, and they do this by designing ever more elaborate coding and frequency-switching systems. A potential enemy then has to try to crack the latest codes. The usual way to obtain samples of secretly coded signals and sophisticated radar transmissions is to eavesdrop.

Both East and West use specially adapted aircraft for the purpose of gathering Electronic Intelligence (Elint) and Communications Intelligence (Comint). One could also use ordinary spies, but spying from the air without over-flying the other side's territory is much easier, and very commonplace even in so-called peacetime. In one recent year alone, the RAF intercepted over 200 Soviet long-range aircraft (mostly Tu-16 and Tu-142 types) which had penetrated UK airspace. From the bulges and blisters on these aircraft it is possible to guess the nature of the aerials and sensors carried and

17 The world's fastest aeroplane is the Lockheed SR-71 Blackbird, used for strategic reconnaissance, which can fly at more than 1740 knots (2000mph) at altitudes of more than 85,000ft (26,000m). (*Photograph courtesy Lockheed*)

to assume that they were engaged on electronic spying and other reconnaissance tasks.

Reconnaissance

It is said that time spent on reconnaissance is never wasted, but there is more to aerial reconnaissance than simply taking photographs using visible light. Emissions in the invisible *infra-red* part of the spectrum can be detected at night and even through cloud. Most infra-red radiation comes from hot or at least warm, objects and can be used to detect moving vehicles, such as tanks or helicopters, from the heat they produce. At night and in bad weather it is also possible to carry out useful reconnaissance using radar wavelengths.

An aircraft intended for reconnaissance has to be able to survive, and to do this it can choose to rely on speed. some reconnaissance aero-

18 Maintainability. Access panels on the F-15 Eagle. (*Photograph courtesy McDonnell-Douglas*)

planes are specialized versions of fighter aircraft, such as the RF-4 versions of the Phantom, or an equally specialized version of the MiG-25. This is a very fast aeroplane indeed, capable of Mach 3 for short periods. By way of comparison, the US Air Force operates the Lockheed SR-71 Blackbird, an odd-looking aeroplane dedicated to strategic reconnaissance, and capable of burning along at Mach 3 for one and a half hours at a time.

THE GROUND ENVIRONMENT

Air bases need to provide runways, fuel, ammunition and equipment stores, a control tower, radar, navigation and landing aids, missile defences, crew quarters, briefing and planning facilities, etc. Airfields are vulnerable, quite apart from the runways, and arguments rage over the virtues and practicalities of 'dispersing' tactical aircraft to secondary bases, such as grass airstrips or stretches of road and motorway. The Harrier family needs no runways, Jaguars can operate from grass and Tornadoes can use damage-shortened runways or even taxiways. Short Take-Off and Landing (STOL) ability is beginning to be recognized as a vital requirement for any future generation of tactical aircraft.

19 Dutch technicians working on an F-16 in a Hardened Aircraft Shelter. (*Photograph courtesy Koninklijke Luchtmacht*)

Whether on a permanent airfield or dispersed to some temporary base, the ground environment must provide all manner of support facilities, such as C³I mentioned earlier (*see p.25*). Besides support facilities, there are other equally important, though less tangible 'abilities': survivability in the event of a surprise attack, reliability in all weather conditions, impenetrability (for example by terrorists, etc.) and serviceability.

During the Falklands War the Royal Navy was able to maintain 90 per cent of its aircraft at full combat-readiness in all weathers, working by torchlight at night or on a freezing flight-deck in an Antarctic gale. Gone are the days when a malfunctioning piece of equipment, such as a radar, needed attention by skilled technicians with screwdrivers and soldering irons. Built-in Test Equipment (BITE) helps to locate faults quickly, and, if components are designed as plug-in LRUs (Line Replaceable Units), the faulty part can be interchanged quickly for a spare by a technician wearing NBC gloves. Compared to civil aircraft, military planes have always seemed to need a lot of maintenance between flights, but the latest fighters are able to fly repeated sorties with little more than refuelling, re-arming and a cursory visual inspection between flights.

2 Flying Machines

I am working on the assumption that the reader has some understanding of conventional aeroplanes. They fly because the wings produce lift as they are pushed forward through the air, and the heavier the aeroplane, the more lift the wings have to produce. The wings, and for that matter all other external parts of the aeroplane, incur a drag penalty as they move through the air. This drag, or air resistance, increases with speed, and the more powerful the engines, the more drag they can overcome and the faster the plane will fly. The plane is controlled by rudder pedals and a joystick, although this latter isn't always a 'stick'. On larger aircraft it is termed a 'control column wheel' or 'yoke', depending on its shape. Pulling back on the joystick tends to make the plane climb, pushing it forward starts a dive, and rocking it from side to side causes the plane to bank (or roll).

It isn't necessary for a pilot to hang on grimly to the controls at all times, ready to correct instantly the smallest deviation from the plane's intended course or altitude. Conventional aeroplanes possess a fair amount of built-in stability. The fin keeps the plane flying straight; the horizontal tail keeps it flying level, and the usual arrangement here is to design the plane nose-heavy and to balance this out by having the tail produce a downforce. Should the plane dive, the speed will increase and so will the downforce on the tail, correcting the dive and restoring the plane to level trim. Any tendency for the plane to roll on to one wingtip will also be counteracted by a complex interaction between the fin and the wings.

PAYLOAD VERSUS RANGE

Most military aircraft are not very different from commercial types. A fighter-bomber can be considered to be like a transport aircraft in that its primary purpose is to carry a payload from A to B using as little fuel as possible. Other things being equal, fuel economy is what determines range or combat radius. Fuel is heavy and, the more fuel a plane needs the fewer the bombs it can carry. This is the *payload versus range* dilemma.

In practical terms, the payload/range dilemma is typified by the pylons under a fighter-bomber's wings. Bombs, rockets or missiles can be attached to these, and so can extra fuel tanks. Fuel tanks hook on in the same way as bombs, and if necessary they can be dropped in an emergency or when they are empty. So the pilot, or whoever makes the decisions, has a choice: fuel tanks for extra range or more bombs for extra striking power. Either way, nobody can risk exceeding the aircraft's permitted 'all-up', or Maximum Take-Off Weight (MTOW). If one did, one would run out of concrete before the plane could stagger into the air at the minimum speed at which it would fly safely.

Lift from the Wings

Military transport aircraft have long, straight, efficient and powerful wings on which it is easy to incorporate a variety of high-lift devices,

20 Airflow over a wing. (A) At normal shallow angles of attack the airflow is bent down over the upper surface of the wing. (B) Close to the stall this ceases to happen and turbulence results. (C) These effects can be defeated by using slats and flaps to keep the airflow attached to a wing at a high angle of attack, bending the airflow down over the back of the wing once more. (D) Similarly, on high-performance, tactical aircraft, stalling can be averted by increasing the wing's camber and by using vortex-inducing LERX.

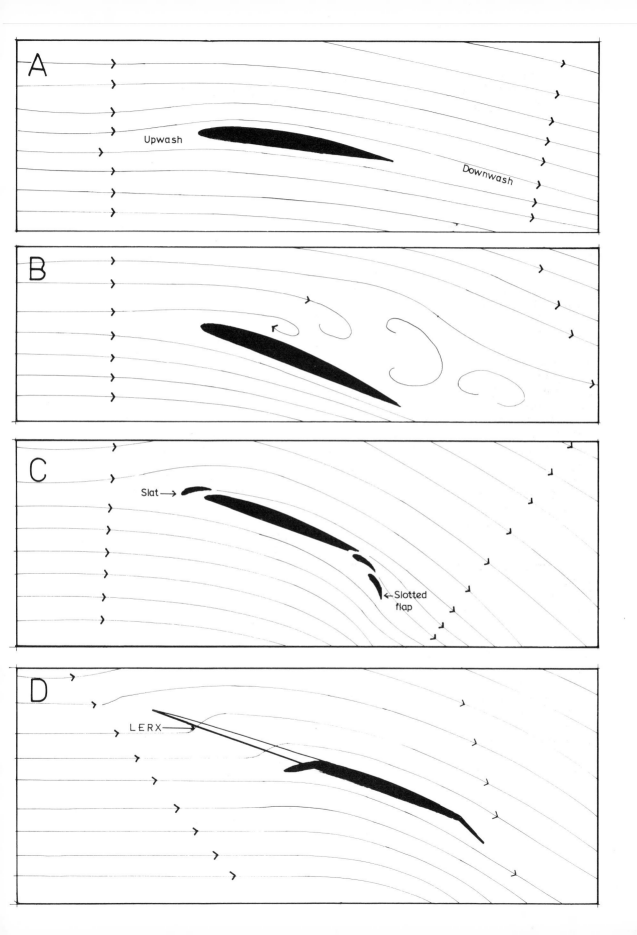

such as flaps and slats, designed to improve the wing's lifting ability at low speeds. Even with a full load, a Hercules, Short Skyvan, Aeritalia G-222 and many other tactical transports can take off and land in a short distance, and this is particularly important where runways are damaged, in poor condition or non-existent.

The wing's lifting ability depends on its aerofoil shape. Airflow over a typical aerofoil section is shown in Fig. 20 and lift is produced by the pressure difference between the airflow above and below the wing. The airflow passing over the top of the wing is speeded up, because it has to travel farther, and this produces low pressure above and higher pressure below. The more the airflow is required to bend, the more energy is imparted to it, and this energy is realised as *lift*, pushing upwards on the wing and supporting the weight of the aircraft. Extra lift can be obtained by using a fatter and more curved aerofoil section, by fitting a bigger wing, by flying faster, or by increasing the wing's *angle of attack*.

Angle of Attack

There are several situations in which a wing will be required to work harder and to produce extra lift. A heavily laden aircraft is an obvious example, but it is necessary for a plane to be able to fly at fairly low speeds, particularly to keep the landing and take-off distances short. When flying slowly a plane needs to compensate for the low airspeed over the wings by holding the nose up so that the aerofoil meets the airflow at a higher angle of attack. This works up to a certain point, beyond which the angle of attack cannot be increased any further without a *stall* occurring. When an aerofoil stalls, the airflow is no longer bent downwards over the top of the wing, but breaks away into turbulent eddies. Drag increases dramatically and most of the lift is suddenly lost. A plane which was flying slowly in a nose-up attitude a moment ago now pitches downwards into a dive. A wing which is fitted with high-lift devices, such as trailing-edge flaps or leading-edge slats, will perform as though it were a much fatter more curved aerofoil at low speeds, producing much more lift and delaying the onset of stall until a lower airspeed or a higher angle of attack is reached.

The air in which aeroplanes fly decreases in density and pressure the higher a plane climbs. Airline passengers hurtling through the air in a pressurized tube 35,000ft (10,000m) above sea level, rarely consider what the air outside their cabin windows is doing. Apart from racing past at close to 500 knots (575mph), its pressure is less than one quarter of that at sea level, its density is less than one-third, and it is freezing cold: minus 54°C. The low density reduces both lift and drag. To keep the plane flying level the pilot has to fly in a somewhat nose-up attitude (high angle of attack) and the stewardesses complain about having to push their trolleys uphill. But the reduced drag is a bonus: high speeds are possible on only a fraction of the power which would be required lower down; fuel burn is greatly reduced, and much longer ranges (and combat radii) are possible than if a plane were to fly at low altitude. The only limiting factor may be the speed of sound.

Approaching Mach One

Sound consists of pressure waves travelling in air. At sea level these pressure waves travel at 662 knots (762mph) under typical conditions. In the cold air of higher altitudes the speed of sound drops with temperature until it remains constant at about 574 knots (661mph) from about 36,000ft (about 11,000m) upwards. An aircraft flying close to the speed of sound (Mach 1.0) is beginning to overtake its own pressure waves which cannot now escape ahead of the aircraft. Instead, 'shock waves' build up which interfere with the airflow over the wings and control surfaces, sometimes producing a disturbing phenomenon known as 'Mach buffet'. Because the airflow over the wings is speeded up by the aerofoil, this can exceed Mach 1.0 even though the plane is flying well below this speed. As most people appreciate, the onset of Mach buffet and other transonic effects can be delayed by various means, usually by sweeping the wings backwards.

Swept wings always result in some loss of wing efficiency. There is less lift and more drag, and stronger, wasteful vortices or whirlpools of air are produced by the wing tips. High-lift devices, such as slats and flaps, work much less well on wings that are swept back. There is even a tendency to abandon sweepback in favour of

21 Tupolev Tu-22 (NATO reporting codename BLINDER) medium-range reconnaissance bombers show off their swept wings and sharply pointed noses. The Tu-22 is capable of Mach 1.4 at 40,000ft (12,000m). (*Photograph via RAF*)

other solutions to the 'sound barrier' problem. One such solution is a razor-sharp wing, as on the Lockheed Starfighter. Another solution, which does not get rid of sweepback altogether but which enables it to be much reduced, is the so-called 'supercritical', or as it is more correctly termed, 'aft-loaded' aerofoil. This spreads the lift which is produced towards the back of the wing, resulting in a more controlled build-up of airspeed over the top surface, and a consequent delaying of Mach effects without the need for excessive sweepback. Two familiar aeroplanes which use aft-loaded aerofoil sec-

tions are the British Aerospace Hawk and the Airbus range of airliners.

Sweepback is still necessary for high supersonic speeds, and with sweepback goes the familiar pointed nose plus a variety of strange 'waisted' shapes for fuselages and air intakes, particularly on aircraft designed for low-level tactical missions or for combat flying.

WINGS FOR COMBAT AIRCRAFT

The high power available from reheated jet engines makes flight at truly supersonic speeds an everyday capability of many present-day military aircraft. These speeds, up to Mach 2.0 and beyond, are only possible in the thin air of high altitude and, in practice, this means being clearly visible to hostile radars. Very few aircraft are capable of *low-level* supersonic flight,

altitude), but with wings unswept and dangling full-span flaps and slats, the Tornado can get airborne with a full bombload from a runway of about ½ mile (just under 1km) or land and stop dead within less than 1200ft (about 365m) using its airliner-type thrust reversers.

The idea of using VG wings dates back to the World War II inventor Barnes Wallis, but the first combat aircraft to be built with them, the General Dynamics F-111, suffered teething troubles, and many designers shied away from the concept, preferring to stay with fixed wings of various styles. On tactical aircraft these were usually swept back, and stubby in order to reduce the stresses of low-level, high-speed flight.

The Anglo-French SEPECAT (Société Européenne de Production d'Ecole de Combat et d'Appui Tactique) Jaguar is a good example of a fast jet designed for low-level ground attack and featuring moderately swept, short, stubby wings. Much lift is lost and drag produced by the strong vortices which spill from the tips of such wings, and in humid conditions these vortices show up as vapour trails.

Short, stubby wings have other disadvantages too. They are not usually long enough for flaps and ailerons of the conventional type to be fitted and, should the designer desire long, powerful flaps which will reduce the take-off and landing run substantially, he will have to exercise some ingenuity. The problem can be overcome by getting one control surface to do the job of two. Flaps can be extended to the wingtip and roll control provided by means other than ailerons. If the outer sections of the flaps can move differentially to provide roll control, they are termed 'flaperons', and if the spoiler-type airbrakes fitted on top of the wings can move differentially, then we have 'spoilerons'. A third solution is to fit a differentially moving tail, i.e. 'tailerons', as in the case of the Tornado.

High-lift devices fitted to wings can have uses other than for landing and taking-off. They can be designed to take high stresses and programmed to deploy whenever high lift is needed, for example in air combat. When a fighter turns it banks over and uses its wings to pull it round the turn. Pulling a tight turn during combat can bring a fighter's wing dangerously close to the stall. The Phantom, miracle fighter of

22 Flypast by RAF Tornado GR.1s with wings at different angles of sweep

partly because of the increased air density and partly because of the turbulence which is invariably present near the ground. The combination of high turbulence and Mach buffet puts severe stresses on an airframe.

But this is where Variable Geometry (VG), or swing wings, score. Planes such as the F-111, Tornado, Sukhoi Su-24, and MiG-23 can take off and land with their wings in the high-lift, unswept position, then angle their wings backward either for high-altitude supersonic flight or for ground-hugging flight at high subsonic speeds. Planes like Tornado which can transform themselves into long slim paper darts enjoy a much better ride at low level, partly because of advanced control systems but partly because the crew are seated well forward of the wing, away from the worst of the turbulence and buffeting. Tornado in particular makes the best of several worlds. With its wings fully swept back it is the fastest aeroplane in the world at low level (Mach 1.2 plus at treetop height!) and one of the fastest at any level (Mach 2.2 at

23 Showing clearly in the humid conditions, vortices spill from the tips of a Jaguar's wings. (*Photograph courtesy British Aerospace*)

the 'sixties, found itself being outmanoeuvred by the MiG-21 during Vietnam dogfights. Despite the Phantom's power and weight, the lightly loaded wing of the MiG pulled much better in turns. Superiority was restored to the Phantom with the appearance of the F-4E version with leading-edge slats. These delayed the stall and made tighter sustained turns possible as well as improving landing performance.

Delta Wing

The delta wing is a logical development of swept-wing technology. Some deltas have tails (Gloster Javelin, MiG-21), but on a classic delta, such as the Vulcan or the Mirage, the trailing edge of the wing functions as a tail, providing a dynamic download to balance the plane's nose-heaviness. The moving control surfaces operate together as elevators but differentially as ailerons, and are termed 'elevons'. There are no flaps.

The true delta, Mirage-style, provides a simple and elegant solution to some of the jet fighter's structural problems because the long wing root can be made deep enough to produce a light but sturdy wing/fuselage joint and also thousands of litres of internal fuel tankage. Marcel Dassault's Mirage deltas have sold (and fought) successfully all over the world.

There are, however, some disadvantages. With no flaps to reduce the landing speed, the early Mirages came in at 180 knots (207mph) and needed a lot of runway on which to stop. A similar drawback was apparent in air combat, because Mirages were not able to sustain a tightly pulled turn for very long before the high drag brought them dangerously close to stalling. At one point Dassault abandoned the delta layout and produced the more conventional Mirage F1, somewhat like an overgrown Jaguar, but now the Mirage deltas are staging a comeback. The Mirage 2000 and 4000 have considerably more power than their predecessors and are able to pull a sustained turn without much loss of speed. Moving the wings forward has removed the wasteful downforce on the rear section of the wing, allowing it to work

24 A Saab J35 Draken landing. The vortex lift produced by the unique 'double delta' wing enables the Draken to touch down in a high nose-up attitude without stalling. Note the rear jockey-wheels touching down first. (*Photograph courtesy Saab–Scania*)

harder in a turn and a computerized fly-by-wire system replaces the missing stability and control. Finally, the latest Mirages have automatic leading-edge slats which extend at low speeds and high angles of attack to produce a more curved (cambered) wing, directing the airflow closer to the top of the aerofoil, reducing drag and delaying the stall. This type of automatic slat, varying the camber of the wing, is becoming almost standard on the latest jet fighters, and the next logical step is the flexibly cambered wing, which changes its shape smoothly without any hinges or gaps to break the line of the airflow: the Mission Adaptive Wing (MAW) as it is called.

Vortex Lift

The Concorde airliner is also a true delta, but its unique ogee-shaped wing behaves differently from the Mirages, and the Concorde is not troubled by the same very high landing speeds. Swooping in elegantly in the now familiar nose-high attitude, vortices are produced along the full length of the wings' leading edges, spreading outwards from the under surfaces and, curling over the top, they achieve the useful

objective of keeping the airflow attached to the top of the wing. This is a good case of 'robber turned policeman'. It is known as *vortex lift* and produces a safe landing at moderate speed, without the assistance of flaps.

Vortex lift produced by the intake strakes of Saab's J35 Draken 'double delta' fighter enables it to land and take off at high angles of attack without stalling. The Draken comes in with the nose so high that a pair of jockey wheels needs to be fitted under the tail. In the case of the Draken's successor, the J37 Viggen, vortex lift is produced by a pair of canard foreplanes, and progressively larger and larger canards are beginning to sprout on the newer Mirages, particularly the Mirage III NG (Nouvelle Generation) and its inspiration, the Israeli-designed Kfir (itself a modified Mirage).

New Fighter Developments

The General Dynamics F-16 Fighting Falcon appeared in 1974 and soon established itself as a superlative air-to-air fighter. It is outstandingly manoeuvrable and agile, thanks partly to the vortex-lift-producing strakes positioned forward of the wings, sometimes called LERX (Leading Edge Root Extensions). These, together with the camber-varying, automatic, leading-edge slats, make the F-16 capable of very tight turns indeed. The under-fuselage air intake overcomes the problem of air **starvation**

25 This static view of a Draken shows the jockey-wheels clearly. (*Photograph courtesy Saab-Scania*)

26 Latest of a long line of delta-winged Mirages, the Super Mirage 4000 shows off its leading-edge slats and canard foreplane. (*Photograph courtesy Avions Marcel Dassault-Breguet Aviation*)

27 Saab J-37 Viggen of the Swedish Air Force, the best example of a canard delta configuration. (*Photograph courtesy Saab-Scania*)

28 F-16 fighter of the Royal Netherlands Air Force. (*Photograph courtesy Koninklijke Luchtmacht*)

29 A carrier-based McDonnell-Douglas F/A-18 Hornet. Both this new fighter design and the F-16 feature 'strake-trapezoidal' wings, with long sharp-edged strakes called LERX forward of the wings. These are intended to delay the stall during tight combat maneouvres. (*Photograph courtesy McDonnell-Douglas*)

at high angles of attack. Some of these features have been copied by new fighters which have appeared since or are still on the drawing board: the F/A-18 Hornet, the F-20 Tigershark, Sweden's JA39 Gripen, and Israel's Lavi. The last two are canard deltas. So too will be the new 'Eurofighter' which is to meet the future needs of Britain, France, Germany, Italy, and Spain.

The F-16 is, of course, the fighter which has been chosen for licence-building by no less than four European air forces: Netherlands, Belgium, Denmark and Norway. This has enabled the manufacturers to consider launching a Multi-Staged Improvement Programme in which the F-16s will be progressively updated and improved (mainly by fitting new avionics), and it has even been shown to be possible to convert the original airframe into a cranked arrow delta which brings considerable benefits to payload/range performance and to manoeuvrability.

PROPULSION

The job of the engines is to provide the power for flight by pushing (or pulling) the plane forward. The airflow thus generated passes over the wings to produce lift. Two engines are always safer than one; if one engine fails a plane should always be able to limp home on the remaining engine or engines, even the worst possible case; an engine failure just after take-off, need not lead to a disaster.

The Propeller

People who are taught to fly on light, single-engined aircraft, such as Pipers or Cessnas, are

amazed to learn that, unlike their family cars, these aeroplanes have no clutch or gearbox; the propeller is simply splined on to the end of the crankshaft. But the angle at which the propeller is set, its 'pitch', is, in effect, a form of gearing and, on the simplest aeroplanes, a fixed propeller pitch will have to be a compromise between different flight requirements: fine pitch (low gear) for take-off versus coarse pitch (high gear) for high-speed cruise at altitude. In practice, all but the simplest propeller-driven aeroplanes have variable pitch, and in most cases this takes the form of automatically varying pitch control, so that whatever the demands on the engine, the revs-per-minute remain constant.

Jet Engines

The propeller remains an efficient way of powering aeroplanes at speeds of up to about 300 knots (345mph) or so; beyond this speed the efficiency of the propeller drops off. It is difficult also to design a propeller with enough 'bite' to make the most of the thin air of high altitude. Therefore at speeds above 300 knots (345mph) and at altitudes above 25,000ft (about 7600m), the jet or gas-turbine engine is best.

In a gas-turbine engine, the energy obtained by burning fuel (usually a form of kerosene) mixed with compressed air causes a large volume of hot gas to be produced. The air is compressed to a ratio of around 22:1 and the hot gas (at up to about 1500°C) drives a turbine shafted to a rotary compressor. It is this multi-staged compressor which sucks in the air at the front of the engine and progressively builds up the pressure to the required amount.

Turbojets

The power produced by a jet engine can be utilized in various ways. The earliest versions were what we now call *turbojets*: all the air which entered at the front of the engine was compressed and forced through the engine's

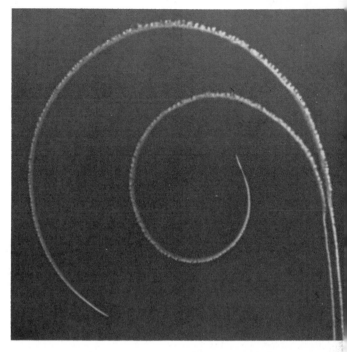

32 Turning ability. A General Dynamics F-16 Fighting Falcon and a slatted F-4E Phantom both entered a tight turn at the same moment. The F-16 finished up well on the inside of the turn. (*Photograph courtesy General Dynamics*)

33 A stretched F-16 with a 'cranked arrow' delta wing. (*Photograph courtesy General Dynamics*)

30 and 31 Two photographs showing how the F-16 manages tight pull-ups and turns without stalling. Vapour trails spill from the strakes and the increased wing camber resulting from the use of flaps and leading-edge slats can be clearly seen. (*Photograph courtesy General Dynamics*)

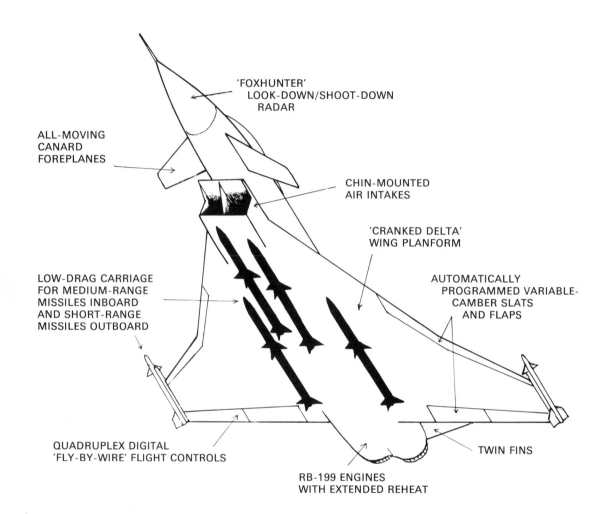

'FOXHUNTER'
LOOK-DOWN/SHOOT-DOWN
RADAR

ALL-MOVING
CANARD
FOREPLANES

CHIN-MOUNTED
AIR INTAKES

'CRANKED DELTA'
WING PLANFORM

LOW-DRAG CARRIAGE
FOR MEDIUM-RANGE
MISSILES INBOARD
AND SHORT-RANGE
MISSILES OUTBOARD

AUTOMATICALLY
PROGRAMMED VARIABLE-
CAMBER SLATS
AND FLAPS

QUADRUPLEX DIGITAL
'FLY-BY-WIRE' FLIGHT CONTROLS

TWIN FINS

RB-199 ENGINES
WITH EXTENDED REHEAT

34 Five European air forces have agreed their requirements for a new fighter, which could be met by this
British Aerospace design study

hot core. These engines enabled hitherto un-
dreamed of speeds and altitudes to be attained.

Turboprop/Turboshaft

For slower, more pedestrian applications, the
advantages of a gas turbine could be harnessed
very economically by designing a larger or a
second turbine which removed most of the
power from the stream of hot exhaust gases and
used it to drive a propeller (*turboprop*) or
helicopter rotor (*turboshaft*) through a reduc-
tion gearbox.

Turbofan

For civil airliner applications, the *by-pass* or
turbofan engine was developed. In this type of
jet engine a large fan takes the place of the first
compressor stage and propels most of the air
around the outside of the core rather than
through it. This arrangement combines the high
cruising speeds of the turbojet with the economy of a turboprop, and is also quieter and
cleaner.

35 The Northrop F-20 Tigershark is a private venture
American fighter designed primarily for export and based
on the successful F-5 series which it closely resembles.
(*Photograph courtesy Northrop*)

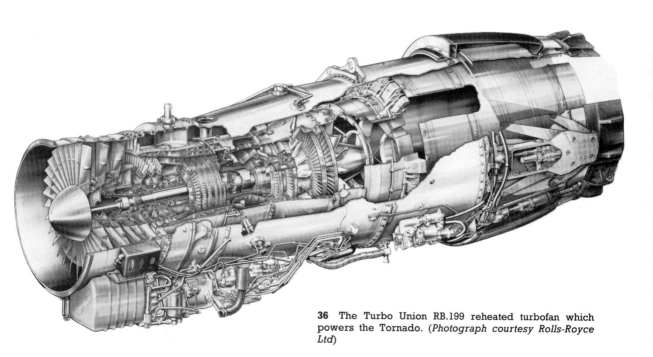

36 The Turbo Union RB.199 reheated turbofan which
powers the Tornado. (*Photograph courtesy Rolls-Royce
Ltd*)

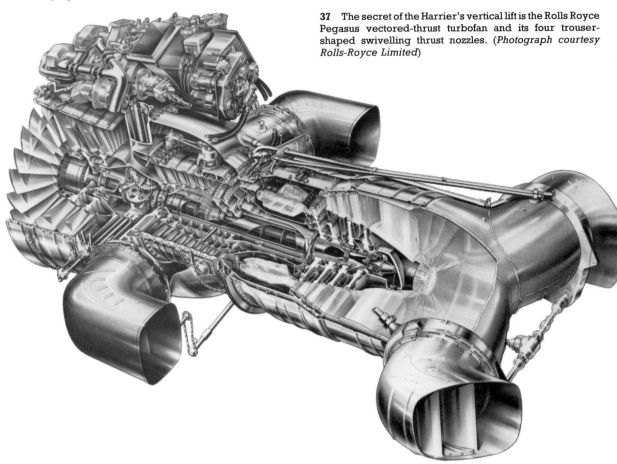

37 The secret of the Harrier's vertical lift is the Rolls Royce Pegasus vectored-thrust turbofan and its four trouser-shaped swivelling thrust nozzles. (*Photograph courtesy Rolls-Royce Limited*)

Vectored-Thrust Turbofan

Finally, the ultimate application of the gas-turbine is the *vectored-thrust turbofan*, such as the Pegasus, which powers the Harrier. In this engine the hot gases from the core of the engine are exhausted through swivelling nozzles which can be turned by the pilot to point downwards for vertical or short take-off. A corresponding amount of thrust is generated by the large fan at the front end of the engine, and the air compressed by it is vectored through two more swivelling nozzles. When the thrust from all of these nozzles is vectored downwards, the Harrier is lifted on four jets of air, producing a combined thrust equal to more than 1.2 times the weight of the plane.

Fighter Powerplants

The Turbo-Union (Rolls-Royce and MTU) RB.199 military turbofan engine developed specially for the Tornado is typical of the latest engines used in tactical aircraft. The RB.199 was developed from the RB.211 civilian turbofan but has a much lower by-pass ratio, 1:1 instead of 5:1. The compression ratio is around 23:1 and the turbine gases circulate at 1327°C at full power. The maximum static thrust is produced by each of the Tornado's two engines. 8000lb (about 3855kg) is boosted to 15,000lb (about 6800kg) by the addition of reheat. Reheat is provided by an afterburner which sprays extra fuel (in considerable quantities) into the hot exhaust gases. Because it uses so much fuel, reheat is only used for take-off and for combat manoeuvring. Without reheat the Tornado GR.1 has a mission radius with full bombload of nearly 900 miles (1440km) (East Anglia to well inside Poland) and the F.2 can loiter on Combat Air Patrol for up to four and a half hours. Both capabilities demonstrate the excellent fuel-efficiency of the RB.199 powerplants.

For maximum jet efficiency, exhaust nozzles change their shape by extending backwards. Rectangular nozzles are being developed which can be used to aid manoeuvring by vectoring the thrust and, being longer, they help to shroud the engine's hot metal innards from the prying eyes of a heat-seeking missile.

The air intakes at the front end of the engine usually conduct the airflow down a long ramp to the compressor. On military aircraft, which fly at a wide range of speeds, some kind of VG intake is useful to ensure a steady airflow, particularly at supersonic speeds. Some MiG-21s have a buffet cone which is motored forward at high speeds, progressively restricting the airflow to the engines (this buffet cone doubles as a radome), and on aircraft such as the F-104 Starfighter and various Mirages there are half-cones (called 'mice') which operate in the same way. A large baffle-plate forward of the intake on, for example a Phantom, is called a *flow separator*, and its job is to prevent the engine from ingesting air which has been slowed down by friction with the fuselage nose. These, plus the arrangement of rectangular sprung doors fitted to the squared ramps of the Jaguar and Tornado are all ingenious devices to maintain a smooth supply of air to the engines and prevent that most annoying of jet engine bad habits: compressor blade stall.

HELICOPTERS

They may look simple, but helicopters remain among the most complex of flying machines, with much of the complexity packed into the hinges and levers which festoon the rotor blade hub. Lifting off is straightforward enough. By the pilot's left hand is the collective pitch lever. When he pulls on this, it increases the pitch of all the rotor blades and their 'bite' on the air. An automatic throttle makes sure that the rotor rpm remains constant, and the helicopter lifts off into the hover. What is amazing to many people is

that the rotor blades are free to flap up and down; what keeps them stretched out in a flat disc is centrifugal force.

The tail rotor on a helicopter is there to prevent the fuselage twirling round as a result of engine torque. A quick blip by the pilot on the rudder pedals changes the pitch of the tail rotor and the helicopter changes direction. But the main control in the pilot's hands is the cyclic pitch lever, which is free to move forward or back, or from side to side. One push forward and the helicopter 'translates' into forward flight, but this is anything but a simple process.

Pushing the cyclic pitch lever forward causes each rotor in turn to increase its pitch as it passes the tail of the helicopter and to decrease pitch as it passes the nose. The plane of the rotor disc now tilts forward, pulling the helicopter after it until it moves away in a nose-down attitude. In forward flight, one blade is advancing, the other retreating. The advancing blade is moving faster through the air and, as a result, is generating more lift. Either the cyclic pitch control is used to lower the pitch of the advancing blade to compensate, or the blade's natural flexibility achieves the same result automatically.

The procedures for flying helicopters seem to have been derived from fixed-wing practice. They land and take off using runways and fly circuits similar to ordinary aircraft, descending at an angle to within a few feet of the ground before finishing the descent vertically. If a helicopter were to descend a long way vertically, it would be flying through its own rotor downwash, which would be inadvisable. In the event of engine failure, a helicopter can de-clutch its rotors and 'glide' or 'autorotate' like a falling sycamore seed. The trouble is that it takes quite a lot of sky to get established in autorotational descent and, as military helicopters fly very low, they are likely to fall like a stone if they are hit during a battle. Military helicopters need to be designed so that they can survive a crash from about 20ft (about 6m) without injuring the occupants.

On a military helicopter the tail rotor is vulnerable, and a number of ideas are being experimented with to replace it with an air jet or some other device which will continue working safely despite a few bulletholes. The Russians use titanium armour to protect their helicopters

PANAVIA TORNADO F.2

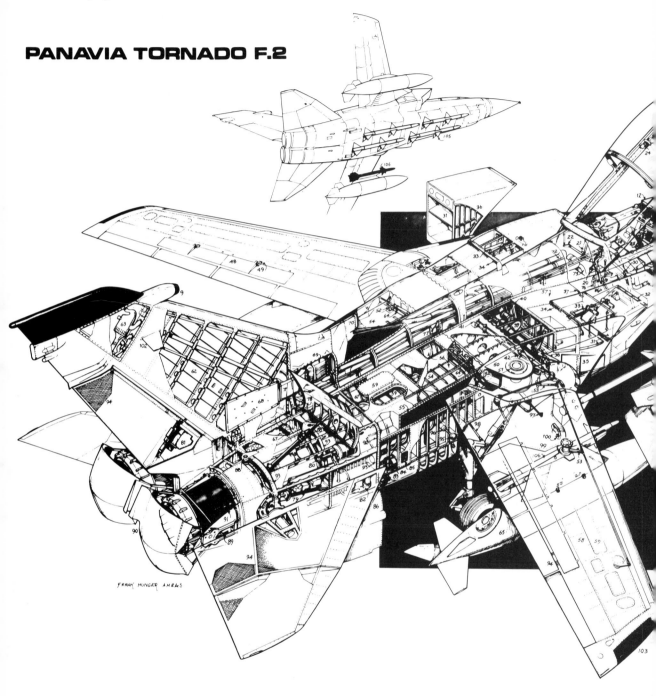

FRANK MUNGER AMRAeS

38 Panavia Tornado F.2 cutaway. (*Courtesy Flight International*)

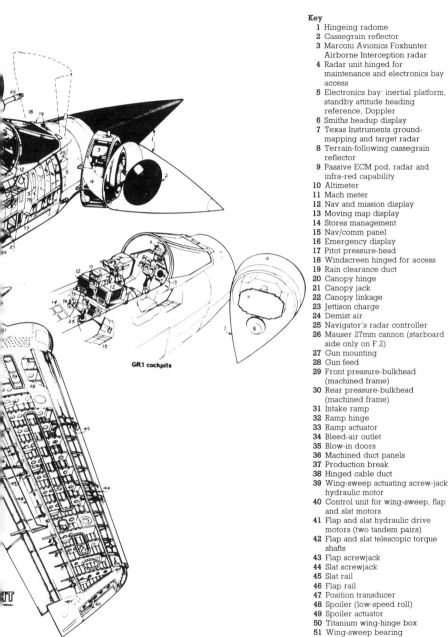

GR.1 cockpits

Key

1 Hingeing radome
2 Cassegrain reflector
3 Marconi Avionics Foxhunter Airborne Interception radar
4 Radar unit hinged for maintenance and electronics bay access
5 Electronics bay: inertial platform, standby attitude heading reference, Doppler
6 Smiths headup display
7 Texas Instruments ground-mapping and target radar
8 Terrain-following cassegrain reflector
9 Passive ECM pod, radar and infra-red capability
10 Altimeter
11 Mach meter
12 Nav and mission display
13 Moving map display
14 Stores management
15 Nav/comm panel
16 Emergency display
17 Pitot pressure-head
18 Windscreen hinged for access
19 Rain clearance duct
20 Canopy hinge
21 Canopy jack
22 Canopy linkage
23 Jettison charge
24 Demist air
25 Navigator's radar controller
26 Mauser 27mm cannon (starboard side only on F.2)
27 Gun mounting
28 Gun feed
29 Front pressure-bulkhead (machined frame)
30 Rear pressure-bulkhead (machined frame)
31 Intake ramp
32 Ramp hinge
33 Ramp actuator
34 Bleed-air outlet
35 Blow-in doors
36 Machined duct panels
37 Production break
38 Hinged cable duct
39 Wing-sweep actuating screw-jack hydraulic motor
40 Control unit for wing-sweep, flap and slat motors
41 Flap and slat hydraulic drive motors (two tandem pairs)
42 Flap and slat telescopic torque shafts
43 Flap screwjack
44 Slat screwjack
45 Slat rail
46 Flap rail
47 Position transducer
48 Spoiler (low-speed roll)
49 Spoiler actuator
50 Titanium wing-hinge box
51 Wing-sweep bearing
52 Wing-box to fuselage link (front and rear)
53 Pylon alignment linkage
54 Wing-sweep cavity
55 Bleed-air-inflated seal
56 Engine intake duct
57 Forward fuel tank
58 Wing tank
59 Tank access
60 Fuel vent
61 Aft fuselage tank
62 Fin fuel tank
63 Fuel jettison and vent system
64 Telescoping fuel lines
65 Pylon tank (330 Imp gal)
66 Inflight-refuelling probe
67 Engine bleed duct
68 Heat shield
69 Bleed-air pre-cooler for air conditioning
70 Ram-air inlet
71 Ram-air exhaust
72 Bleed-air to air-conditioning units (lower fuselage)
73 Equipment cooling air
74 Pitch control linkage
75 Roll control linkage
76 Pitch and roll feel and trim linkage
77 Pitch and roll nonlinear gearing
78 Pitch and roll linkage to tailplane
79 Tailplane actuator; differential for roll
80 Hydraulic reservoir (both sides)
81 Rudder actuator (electrically signalled)
82 Hydraulic filters
83 Accessory drive gearbox
84 Auxiliary power unit (APU)
85 APU exhaust
86 Engine access doors
87 Turbo-Union RB.199-34R-4 Mk 101 Turbofan engine (8000lb dry, 15,000lb reheat)
88 Engine mounting and winching points
89 Thrust-reverser actuator
90 Reverser buckets deployed
91 Afterburner nozzle actuator
92 Production break/engine-bay bulkhead
93 Forged frame
94 Metal honeycomb filling
95 undercarriage pivot
96 Main jack
97 Door jack
98 Wheel swivel link
99 Door
100 Landing/taxi lamp
101 VHF antenna
102 VOR antenna
103 Wingtip antenna
104 Notch antenna
105 BAe Sky Flash air-to-air missile
106 AIM-9L Sidewinder air-to-air missile

39 Kamov Ka-25 helicopters aboard the *Minsk*. These unique and compact shipboard helicopters feature co-axial, contra-rotating main rotors and no tail rotor. (*Photograph courtesy Fotokhronika Tass*)

40 A Royal Navy Sea Harrier of No. 801 Naval Air Squadron lifts off from the ski-jump of HMS *Invincible*. Without the ski-jump the Sea Harriers would not have been able to respond so effectively to the varying requirements of the Falklands War. (*Photograph courtesy Royal Navy*)

from ground fire, and in the Mi-26 they have the world's heftiest helo, weighing 56 tonnes fully laden as compared with the West's biggest chopper, the Sikorsky CH-53E Super Stallion which weighs in at a mere 33 tonnes MTOW.

Because of difficulties with the advancing blade tip going into Mach buffet, there is a limit to the maximum forward speed helicopters can attain. This is around 174 knots (200mph) in most cases, and there are a number of experimental helicopters undergoing tests to overcome the problem. The Bell XV-15 tilt-rotor demonstrator has reached over 295 knots (340mph), and ABC (Advancing Blade Concept) helicopters have successfully demonstrated the feasibility of mounting two contra-rotating rotor blade sets on the same hub. But this idea is by no means new. The Kamov Ka-25 shipboard helicopter has been flying since 1967 with contra-rotating blades and no tail rotor, and has been the Soviet Navy's main anti-submarine helicopter since about 1970.

THE HABITS OF A HARRIER

Since the Falklands War it has been impossible not to take the Harrier family of aircraft seriously. They have proved themselves as successful combat aircraft and their unique Short Take Off and Vertical Landing (STOVL) capability enables them to operate in and out of situations unthinkable to pilots of more conventional military planes. In May 1983 a royal Navy Sea Harrier successfully made an unscheduled and unheralded landing on top of containers between the masts of a cargo ship plying her normal trade in the Atlantic.

A vertical take-off requires all the rated thrust of the Harrier's Pegasus powerplant, and additional fuel and weapons for improved payload/range can only be carried if the Harrier takes off on a conventional runway or from a ski-jump, rather than vertically. Once flying forward, even a fully laden Harrier can climb away rapidly using its enviable thrust-to-weight ratio. The use of vectored thrust in flight makes it equally as effective as the latest US combat aircraft with their high-lift wings. It can fly slowly without stalling, stand on its tail, and turn almost square corners – all-in-all adding up to the kind of manoeuvring ability which makes the Harrier a formidable opponent in a dogfight.

Even where there is a long runway, a Harrier normally lands by slowing down into the hover, using almost full downward-vectored thrust on its noisy approach. Hovering motionless at below 70ft (about 21m), a Harrier can control its yaw, pitch and roll by using jets of high-pressure bleed-air issuing from the tail, nose and wingtips. Hovering too close to the runway (in ground effect) is not considered safe practice, owing to the risk of ingesting foreign objects blasted up from the ground.

The thrust produced by current versions of the Harrier's Pegasus engine is in the region of 21,500lb. A derivative of this engine is used in the joint McDonnell-Douglas/British Aerospace AV-8B/Harrier II now being produced for the US Marine Corps, the RAF and the Spanish Navy. Later developments may result in a supersonic jump-jet (Advanced STOVL) which will require an even more powerful Pegasus with PCB (Plenum Chamber Burning) to increase further the thrust-to-weight ratio.

3 The Electronic Environment

The electromagnetic spectrum consists of radiations produced by a variety of sources, some natural, others man-made. Hot bodies, such as the sun, radiate energy in the form of heat and light and these are absorbed, reflected, stored or transformed by objects in the environment. Military interest in the electromagnetic spectrum includes both natural and man-made radiation; detecting targets such as tanks and aircraft by the heat they give off, or submarines by the noises they make, or, alternatively, using artificially produced, coherent electromagnetic radiation for such purposes as radio communication, radar and lasers.

RADIO COMMUNICATION

Radio works by producing a series of voltage changes from positive to negative and back again, many times per second in a metal wire, rod or similar (called an *aerial* by the British and an *antenna* by most others). The electromagnetic waves caused in this way spread outwards and produce resonance in aerials connected to similarly tuned circuits. A radio receiver which is tuned to one transmitter's frequency should not resonate at the frequency of another.

Frequencies and Wavelength

The frequencies used by radio are more or less steady, and, because the waves travel outwards at the speed of light (almost exactly 300,000km per second), the length of each wave can be found by dividing the frequency into 3×10^8 metres. Similarly, frequency can be found by dividing wavelength into the same figure. Try this calculation for your favourite radio stations and you will find that it works!

Radio One $= \dfrac{300,000,000 \text{ metres per second}}{275 \quad \text{metres}}$
$= 1,090,909$ waves or cycles per second
$= 1091$ kilohertz (kHz)*

* The published frequency 1089 kHz allows for the average drop in frequency when sound is added.

Frequencies from as low as 10 kHz (wavelength 30km) up to about 300 gigahertz (GHz), 300,000 million cycles per second (wavelength 1mm) are used in radio and radar applications. Up and down this spectrum the properties vary depending upon wavelength and frequency. As frequency is increased, the wavelength shortens and more information can be carried. Aerials can be reduced in size from the immensely long wires needed for the longest waves to short rods of only a few centimetres in length which are sufficient to transmit and receive microwaves, and it then becomes easier to concentrate the signals into a strong directional beam travelling more or less in a straight line.

The radio part of the spectrum is divided into bands ranging from VLF (Very Low Frequency) up to EHF (Extremely High Frequency), according to a conventional classification (*see Fig. 41*). VLF waves cannot be modulated with sound or television signals, but they can transmit telegraphic dots and dashes and they have the important advantage that they curve round the earth, making very long-distance communication and navigation systems possible. As one progresses up the spectrum through the MF

41 Military and other uses of the electromagnetic spectrum

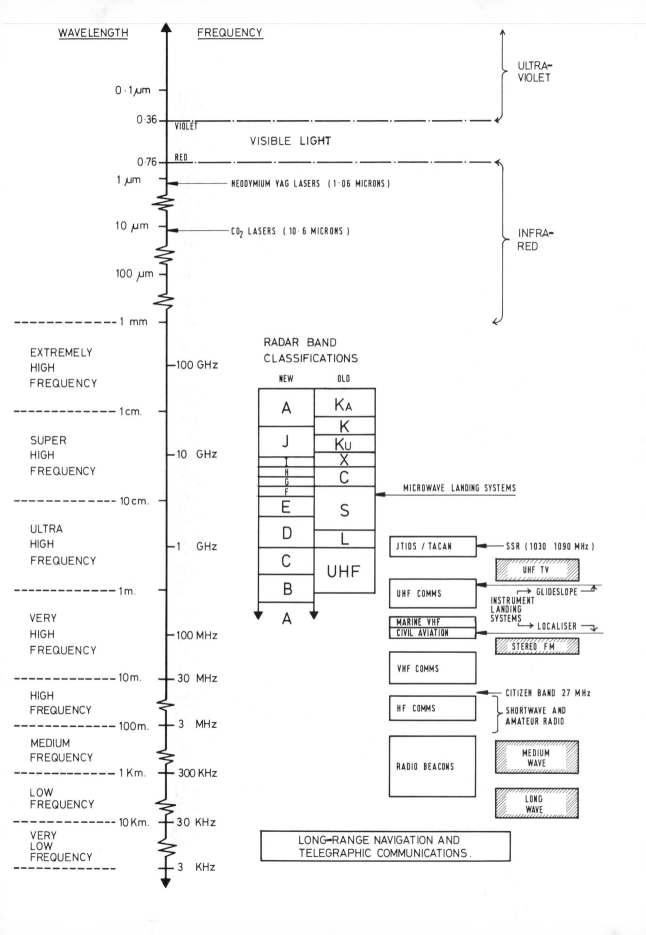

and HF bands, the sky begins to play an increasingly important part in the propagation of radio waves. They are reflected by the layers of charged particles in the ionosphere and, under the right conditions, trans-globe communication is possible using the 'short waves' of the HF band as they bounce off the sky and earth repeatedly, not once but twice or more. HF transmissions are used to communicate with aircraft at long range or which are flying over the oceans.

Wavelengths shorter than 10m (i.e. frequencies above 30 MHz) are not reflected in this way, and pass through the ionosphere. Frequencies in the VHF bands and above travel more or less in straight lines and are not bent round the earth's curvature or reflected over the horizon, but they are suitable for medium-range communication between aircraft and between aircraft and ground stations. Coverage is well over 100 miles (160km) under most conditions and clear, noise-free communication can be enjoyed. The radio transmitter receivers (transceivers) carried by most military aircraft operate at frequencies in the VHF and UHF bands.

Military Radio

Military communication uses a number of different spot frequencies or channels located within a number of frequency bands, each assigned to a different purpose. Ground forces normally use the VHF band from 30–88 MHz and the pilot of a tactical or close-support aircraft needs to be able to maintain contact with this. He will also need to contact the civil air traffic control networks, the civil navigation and landing aids, such as the Instrument Landing Systems (ILS), and shipping and maritime VHF stations. All of these are allocated different parts of the band from 108–174 MHz, and military aviation (that is pilots, airfields and controllers) has its own band containing 7000 spot channels from 225–400 MHz. It is a radio engineer's nightmare to design a transceiver which will work on all of these frequencies and which can still be controlled from a small box that fits within the cramped confines of a tactical aircraft's cockpit. Normally, the pilot selects the channel he wants by 'dialling' the required frequency into the display window. He is then listening in to that channel; if he wishes to transmit he pushes a

button on his control column. There are refinements. For example, most transceivers are permanently listening in on the distress frequencies of 121.5 Mhz (civil) 156.8 MHz (marine) and 243 MHz (military aircraft). In order to save time 'fiddling' when calling up regularly used channels, there is also provision to store up to 20 of the more important frequencies in the radio's memory, although probably, this is a hangover from the more primitive days when airborne radios would only tune in to a limited number of 'stud' channels, each represented by its own tuning crystal.

Electronic Countermeasures (ECM) and Counter-Countermeasures (ECCM)

For every electronic system available to a military power, some kind of countermeasure can be devised. Radio messages can be intercepted by an enemy and 'eavesdropped', 'spoofed' or 'jammed'. Eavesdropping can be prevented by coding the message in some form, and coding also protects against spoofing (i.e. the transmitting of bogus messages or false information). Jamming is, however, the commonest and easiest form of ECM and consists of broadcasting 'noise' using as much power as possible on the frequency of the signal which it is required to jam.

Against every countermeasure there are counter-countermeasures. The most widely used ECCM against high-power noise jamming is 'frequency agility'. Both transmitter and receiver skip from one frequency to another in accordance with pre-arranged codes. Another ECCM is to use a broad band of adjacent frequencies (spread spectrum techniques) which forces the jammer to do likewise. If it is necessary to use one spot frequency, secure voice communication can be obtained by 'encryption' or 'scrambling'. The voice is sampled as a series of pulses which are then transposed according to codes in prearranged keylists programmed into the transmitter's software. At the receiving end the reverse happens and speech emerges once again. Scrambling can be made even more secure if, instead of voice, data or telegraphic signals are used. On board a large aircraft, such as a Nimrod or E-3, a radio teletype machine can be carried. Messages are typed into a keyboard and the replies print out on paper on a machine similar to a Telex.

Joint Tactical Information Distribution (Jtids)

Rather than continually relaying urgent messages from one operator to another, it is possible to devise a system in which everyone is capable of receiving all the information destined for everyone else, and a computer is used to sort out which messages are intended for or of interest to a particular user. This provides the steady flow of up-to-the-minute, reliable information which is vital to anyone fighting a war, provided it can be made secure against enemy interference, which is what NATO's new Joint Tactical Information Distribution System (Jtids) is intended to do.

With Jtids, each user is allocated as many 8-millisecond timeslots as his needs require. The system can handle up to 98,000 users, each of whom is allowed to squeeze a 456-bit message into his timeslot each time it comes round.

42 The RAF's new Nimrod AEW.3 is primarily a flying radar station, able to detect low-flying targets out to 250 miles (400km) and high-flying targets out to twice that distance. The very powerful radar has twin scanners, facing fore and aft and synchronized to scan each hemisphere in turn. The Nimrod can also communicate with a variety of aircraft and ground stations, at present using the NATO datalink 11 secure system, but this will eventually be superseded by Jtids. Full IFF target identification equipment is carried and the Loral ESM pods on the wingtips listen to and classify the different radio and radar emissions received. (*Photograph courtesy British Aerospace*)

A single 12-second 'frame' comprises 1536 timeslots and, after 64 such frames, the computer reshuffles the timeslots. Messages are, of course, digital, consisting of encoded bits, and without access to the computer software, an enemy could neither decipher these multiplexed messages nor plug into the system. Switching the operating frequency around the band from 960–1215 MHz makes Jtids very difficult to noise-jam.

Direction Finding

In more primitive times radio direction finding used to mean turning a loop aerial to locate the direction of the transmitter to which it was tuned but, for many years now, airborne systems have been doing this job completely automatically, displaying the bearing of the transmitter on a flight-deck instrument variously termed Radio Compass, Radio Magnetic Indicator (RMI) or Automatic Direction Finder (ADF).

The main use of radio direction finding is as a navigational aid, and for this reason, most direction finders are designed to receive radio beacons in the LF/MF band (190-1800 kHz). Other applications are mostly maritime. Lifejackets worn by crash and shipwreck survivors can be fitted with a SARBE (Search and Rescue Beacon) device which transmits continuously and automatically on the maritime distress frequency 2182 kHz, and enables Search and Rescue ships or aircraft to find the survivors by homing-in on them using their ADF. Other

homing systems operating at VHF or UHF frequencies are used for tracking Anti-Submarine Warfare (ASW) sonobuoys or by naval helicopters for finding their parent ship.

In emergency, military aircraft tune immediately to the UHF distress frequency of 243 MHz. As soon as an aircraft in distress begins to transmit, the signals are picked up on strategically located direction finders scattered around Britain's military airfields. The bearings of the signals are then relayed to the London Military Air Traffic Control Centre at West Drayton, where the position of the aircraft in distress is immediately pinpointed on a large, illuminated chart. No need to bother with radar. Search, rescue and emergency services can then be alerted.

RADAR

Radar is vital to present-day air power and, because of its importance, whether it is ground-based or airborne, much effort is devoted to ways of beating enemy radars by jamming or deception. This, in turn, leads to great efforts to beat the jammers by designing radars which are ever more sophisticated, powerful and resistant to ECM.

A radar transmits a very powerful pulse of radio energy. Any aircraft or other metal object in the vicinity within line of sight will reflect back a small portion of this energy, allowing its direction and range to be determined. The earliest radars did not have scanning aerials because the frequencies used were too low; consequently, their wavelengths were very long and aerials were large and cumbersome – certainly too cumbersome to be made to rotate. However, the development of the cavity magnetron in 1940 made it possible to generate high-power pulses at SHF frequencies, with wavelengths in the centimetric (microwave) band. These radars could be built to scan and to produce a strongly directional beam which made it possible to detect and locate small objects such as submarine periscopes at sea, or to sketch remarkably detailed radar maps of the terrain over which an aircraft happened to be flying.

There are basically two ways in which a directional radar aerial can be built. Most familiar is the *dipole aerial* at the focus of a par-

aboloid reflecting dish or, alternatively, the dipole can be buried in the transmitter and the radio energy fired at the reflector using a *waveguide* in the form of a hollow, curved horn. More complex electronically, but with a number of important advantages is the flat dish aerial, or *planar array*, which consists of a number of small dipoles mounted side-by-side and end-to-end. The more aerials there are mounted in this manner, the more strongly directional the array, provided that the dipoles are fed in phase with each other. Whichever type of scanner is used, a succession of powerful pulses is transmitted and, in between the pulses, the set is switched to receive.

On the familiar circular radar display, known as a PPI (Plan Position Indicator), echoes returning from reflecting objects are shown as blips in the direction in which the scanner was pointing at the time, and the short time which it takes for an echo to return is displayed as the range from the centre of the screen. The newest radars use a good deal of electronic processing in order to show their information more clearly. Displays can be stabilized if required (with radars on board an aircraft, the display need not revolve as the aircraft turns, it can be held steady as the plane flies, or off-centred on whichever part of the field of view happens to be of most interest). But, whichever display is used, it will show up all the radar echoes which it receives, unless there is some means of filtering out unwanted 'clutter', such as the echoes produced by heavy rain or those being returned from the landscape.

Doppler Shift

Moving targets are those which are of most interest to radar operators and, fortunately, the signal returned by these causes the original frequency to be doppler-shifted as a result of the target's movement. The principle of the Doppler Shift is well known. It is this which causes the sound of an approaching aeroplane to seem higher in pitch than when it has flown past, and the principle has some very important applications in radar and navigation. Stationary targets show no Doppler Shift, therefore these can be filtered out of the radar display, leaving only those which are moving relatively to the scanner showing on the screen. Other methods

43 A traditional airfield radar consisting of the familiar 'orange peel' paraboloid reflector fed by a hollow waveguide horn. In the background is the British Aerospace Jaguar Fly-By-Wire testbed which is having its systems checked for possible interference by the high-powered pulses from the radar. (*Photograph courtesy British Aerospace*)

44 Planar-array antenna for the AR3D ground-based radar system. (*Photograph courtesy Plessey Radar Limited*)

of filtering out unwanted echoes include complex mathematical processing to get rid of rain, and giving a ground-based radar a memory for known ground features, such as buildings, which it can be programmed to ignore.

Radar Jamming

A disadvantage of radar is that even at microwave frequencies it is very difficult to build an array which is perfectly directional, sending and receiving only a perfectly collimated parallel beam. All radars have weaker 'sidelobes', which the jammers try to use.

High-power noise-jamming transmits many

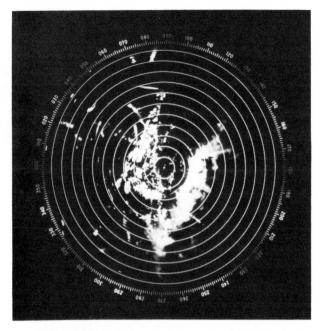
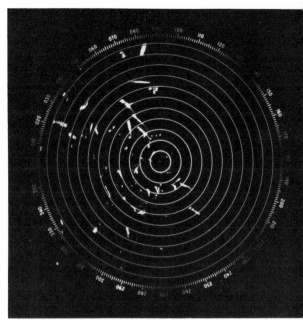

45 Two radar displays. The one on the right has had most of the ground and rain clutter removed by computerized processing of the returned signals. (*Photograph courtesy Plessey Radar Limited*)

times more energy than would be reflected from a normal target, and the jammers hope that this noise will be powerful enough to get through to the receiver via the antenna's low-gain sidelobes at times when the scanner main beam is 'looking' elsewhere. The effect will be to produce a 'white-out' on the radar screen, making it useless for detecting other targets and unable to pinpoint precisely the source of the jamming. Countermeasures against jamming include designing antennae where the sidelobes are very weak or almost non-existent, such as is possible with planar array or Cassegrain-reflecting antennae, but the most important ECCM device is *frequency agility*, i.e. hopping from one frequency to another in order to stay one step ahead of the jammer.

Frequencies and Range

The most suitable carrier wavelengths for radar are those least likely to be affected by atmospheric absorbtion, rain or clouds, but much depends on the actual situation. Ground-based radars tend to prefer the 1-3 GHz band (D, E,

and F bands under the classification, L or S under the old), whereas long-range, airborne radars operate mostly in the I-band (8–12.5 GHz), which was part of the X-band under the old classification. A frequency of 10 GHz has a wavelength of 3cm with good long distance penetration of air and water vapour. Microwaves shorter than 3cm, instead of being reflected by water molecules, tend to be absorbed by them, producing a heating effect. This makes short microwaves ideal for cooking the Sunday joint but useless for long-range radar.

Long-Range Airborne Radar

The range of a ground-based radar extends only slightly farther than the visual horizon. A radar which is only 13ft (4m) above the sea or flat country cannot track a very low-flying target much more than 5 nautical miles (9km) away. In order to track low-flying targets it is necessary to position the radar as high as possible, or better still, get it airborne. An aircraft, such as the Nimrod AEW-3 or the Boeing E-3, is effectively a radar station cruising at 30,000ft (about 9000m), from which altitude it is possible to track low-flying aircraft out to 215 nautical miles (400km) or high-flying targets out to twice that distance.

46 The Grumman F-14 Tomcat was the first fighter to carry powerful long-range pulse-Doppler radar able to look down and detect low-flying targets and to track several targets simultaneously. (*Photograph courtesy US Navy*)

So that radars can operate to these extreme ranges, very high power must be used at the transmitter, and this in turn presents a cooling problem. The Nimrod's radars are liquid-cooled, the waste heat from the coolant being passed in a heat exchanger to the fuel and, as this warm fuel returns to its tanks in the wings, it trickles along channels in the upper wing skin which dissipate the heat to the atmosphere.

Some years ago it would not have been possible to design a radar which could 'look down' and detect moving targets against the cluttered background of echoes returning from the landscape. The principle of the Doppler Shift is used but, in this case, it is necessary to filter out those Doppler-shifted frequencies caused by the parent aircraft moving relative to the ground, and then what remains will be a *different* set of Doppler-shifted frequencies arising from targets moving *over* the ground. Despite the complexity of the signal-processing task, remarkably clean pictures can be pro-duced (*see Fig. 49*). A further complication is that, with such sophisticated Doppler-filtering, it is necessary for the pulses to be *coherent*, that is for the carrier-waveforms of successive pulses to be in phase with each other. A magnetron cannot be used to generate coherent pulses, and it is necessary to use the more complicated Klystron or Travelling Wave Tube (TWT) devices.

There are, however, still more complications connected with long-range airborne radar. A pulse reflected from a target 215 nautical miles (400km) away will take $2\frac{1}{2}$ milliseconds to return and, in theory, the radar should remain in the receiving mode and transmit no further pulses during that time. It seems therefore natural to use a low PRF (Pulse Repetition Frequency) for long-range radar but, in practice, this is not what happens. A rapid succession of long pulses (high PRF) is preferred in order to increase the total energy reflected from the target and make it easier to distinguish from random noise or jamming. The radar is switched to receive only for short intervals between these pulses, and recognizes which incoming pulse is which because successive pulses are transmitted at slightly different fre-

quencies. This provides an electronic label which allows each pulse to be identified correctly on its return, and the range to the target computed.

The Grumman F-14 Tomcat was the first fighter to carry long-range, look-down, pulse Doppler radar when it appeared in the early 'seventies. It also carried a selection of long-, medium- and short-range missiles, each capable of destroying a separate target to which it was guided by the Tomcat's radar and, to do this, the radar had to be able to track targets while continuing to scan. Older radars had to remain locked-on to a target which they were tracking; the scanner remained pointing towards the target and was unable to scan in order to detect or engage other targets. By contrast, the Tomcat's Hughes AN/AWG-9 radar and weapons system continues to scan and uses a computer memory to maintain files on up to 24 separate targets, displaying the position of all of these to the pilot and directing each missile to a separate target if required.

There is, however, a price to pay for this excellence. The Tomcat's AN/AWG-9 radar is heavy and expensive. It processes its Doppler imputs using a bank of nearly 1000 almost identical filtering circuits. Radars designed since then are smaller and lighter and use a much more compact *digital signal processor* in order to analyse the Doppler shifts in the returned echoes. These newer radars are also more flexible. They are what are termed *multimode* radars capable of being switched from any one of several air-to-air modes to an equal number of air-to-ground roles as the mission demands, in each case displaying a different type of information or a different field of view to the pilot.

The F-15 Eagle is equipped with the very adaptable AN/APG-63 radar, the F-16 Fighting Falcon has a Westinghouse APG-66, the F-20 Tigershark has the 'Murphy-proof' APG-67, while what is arguably the best of the new multimode radars, the Hughes APG-65 is mounted in the F/A-18 Hornet. Britain's newest air-to-air radar is the Marconi Avionics/Ferranti Foxhunter of the Tornado F.2, while Thomson-CSF of France is developing new multimode radars for the Mirage 2000 and 4000. Many of these radars use planar-array antennae which produce a directional beam by feeding a large number of dipoles in-phase. Feeding them slightly out-of-phase produces a beam which scans electronically, and this 'phased-array' scanning is used in conjunction with mechanical scanning in some applications.

The Cassegrain aerial provides an alternative to planar arrays. It is named after an early eighteenth-century astronomer who devised a reflecting telescope with two curved mirrors facing each other, and the principle is often

47 The Westinghouse APG-66 radar of the F-16 features a planar array. (*Photograph courtesy General Dynamics*)

48 The Foxhunter radar of the Tornado F.2 showing the housing containing the twisted inverse Cassegrain antenna. (*Photograph courtesy Marconi Avionics*)

49 Photograph of actual radar display from on board a Boeing E-3A of the NATO AEW Force. This shows the very 'clean' picture which is possible using look-down radar with pulse-Doppler filtering to remove unwanted landscape echoes. The symbol representing the parent aircraft is positioned over north Holland and surrounded by a box. Low-flying targets out to 250 miles (400km) can be seen (approximately the distance to London in this picture) and high-flying targets beyond this radius. (*Photograph courtesy NATO AEW Force*)

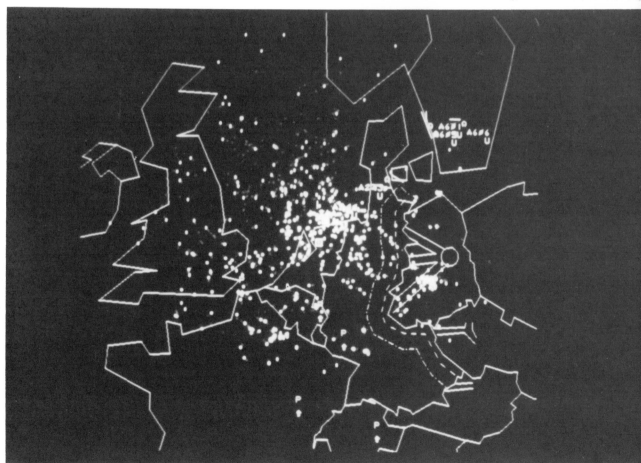

50 Ilyushin Il-18/38 (Coot-A) ECM and Elint-gathering aircraft features SLAR in a long pod under the fuselage.

used in microwave installations. The Antenna of the Foxhunter radar of the Tornado F.2 is of this type, as are the large antennae of the Nimrod AEW3. In both aircraft a pair of slotted reflectors face each other inside a rigid dielectric housing made of glassfibre honeycomb. Signals are fed from waveguides positioned at the centre of the rear reflector. The signals are horizontally polarized and are reflected by the horizontal elements of the front reflector, back to the rear reflector which has elements designed to twist the polarization through 90°. The now vertically polarized signals pass as a parallel beam through the horizontal slots in the front reflector. Just like the planar arrays, the *twisted inverse Cassegrain* antenna arrangement is designed to have a strongly directional main beam and weak sidelobes.

Radar Mapping

Apart from air-to-air combat, airborne radar is also used to provide a detailed map of the terrain over which the aircraft is flying. Such radar maps are useful for navigation, targeting, or as a means of reconnaissance. When used for reconnaissance radar can produce pictures almost as detailed as aerial photographs, regardless of weather conditions, with the added advantage that it is not necessary to overfly possibly hostile targets directly; they can be scanned ahead or to one side. Sharp radar

pictures can only be produced by using a long antenna array in relation to the wavelength, giving a sharp narrow beam with high directional gain. In practice, such an antenna would have to be several metres long and would not fit in the nose of a combat aircraft. It can, however, be fitted along the side or in an underfuselage pod. A Sideways-Looking Airborne Radar (SLR or SLAR) does not need to scan, as the passage of the aircraft can be made to accomplish this. In practice, the radar data is either recorded on tape or transmitted back to the ground station for analysis.

Sharper ground maps can be obtained from a conventionally scanning or nose-mounted airborne radar by adding yet more Doppler signal processing. Any returns which are shown by their Doppler shifts not to have come from the very tip of the beam are filtered out, and the result is termed DBS (Doppler Beam Sharpening) or SAR (Synthetic Aperture Radar).

Interrogators and Transponders

At a civil Air Traffic Control Centre the radar displays are remarkably clean and clutter-free, and each blip is labelled with the aircraft's flight number, registration, 'squawk code' or some other means of identification, plus in most instances a read-out of the aircraft's altitude. This may be very neat and convenient, but how is it done?

The secret is a specialized radar system called Secondary Surveillance Radar (SSR). The radar transmits on 1030 MHz and only listens out for replies on 1090 MHz. Most aircraft carry a device called a *transponder* which listens out for the radar-triggering signal on 1030 MHz and then transmits a coded reply on 1090 MHz. Only aircraft equipped with a suitable transponder can reply in this way, and the system is not affected by reflection from the ground, clouds, etc. for the same reason. The transponder can send all kinds of useful coded information back to the radar, such as a four-digit 'squawk code' inserted by the pilot on instructions from ground control. This squawk can be decoded using a computer to show on the radar as the plane's registration or flight number, and in times of war it serves as an electronic password enabling friend to be distinguished from foe.

In military use, this is the system's most

important function and is termed IFF (Identification, Friend or Foe). Until recently only ground-based operators were able to receive and interpret IFF signals, and the lone fighter pilot up there in the sky had no means of knowing whether the radar target rapidly closing on him was friendly or hostile. Now it is necessary for tactical aircraft to carry their own IFF interrogators and decoders besides the simple transponders carried in the past. This equipment will decode the different squawks (if any) and label the targets on the radar screen as friendly or hostile, according to the official keylist of the day (or the hour), which is programmed into the IFF's software.

Identification is a constant headache for battle commanders. There is a great risk that during a war in Europe, NATO air defences might shoot down their own aircraft, and improved IFF systems are now an urgent requirement, which will be met by the gradual updating of existing equipment to the latest Mk.10 and Mk.12 standards.

ELECTRONIC WARFARE

The details of electronic warfare techniques tend to be kept closely secret; they would be largely meaningless to non-specialists anyway. The broad concepts, however, whether crude or subtle are straightforward enough. Because of the importance of radio, radar and navigation facilities in time of war, a lot of effort is directed towards depriving an enemy of their effective use. Ground-based transmitting and receiving sites can be destroyed by saboteurs, by precision air attacks or by the use of anti-radiation missiles which can home in on radar scanners, communication transmitters, airborne early warning aircraft and even on radar jammers.

Active noise jamming has already been described (*see p. 50*), but in an age of frequency-agile radio and radar systems, there is no point in jamming on one spot frequency only. It is necessary to spread the jamming energy across a broad band of frequencies and even into frequency bands an enemy might not normally be expected to use. By collecting a library of Elint it is possible to build up a very accurate picture of the radio and radar systems a potential enemy might use: their frequencies, frequency-switching habits, radar PRFs and other pulse characteristics, samples of coded signals, and so on. Jamming equipment and techniques can then be designed around this information.

Frequency-agile systems can be defeated by noise-jamming across a range of frequencies, but to do this effectively for each spot frequency in the band, very large amounts of power are required. A new version of the large Ilyushin Il-76 *Candid* transport is designed to carry very powerful generators and noise-jamming transmitters. NATO jamming aircraft, such as the Grumman EA-6 Prowler or the EF-111A Raven are more compact and somewhat less powerful, but these ECM aircraft are officially described as 'tactical jammers', intended to fly closer to the radars they are intended to jam, which would require less power. Other tactical aircraft can carry their own self-protection jamming pods such as the Westinghouse ALQ-101 and 119 pods, or the very sophisticated Marconi Space and Defence Systems 'Sky Shadow' ECM pod which is carried on the outer wing pylons of Tornadoes.

The simplest self-protection ECM device is the Radar Warning Receiver (RWR), and some kind of RWR is fitted to most tactical aircraft, usually in a housing on top of the fin. Early versions of RWR simply warned the pilot by means of a flashing light or a tone in his headset – intermittent for a scanning radar and continuous when the radar ceased scanning and locked on in the tracking mode. Newer RWRs display on a small screen the direction and nature of several radar threats, while the Tornado F.2 will carry a very precise homing-type of RWR, enabling it not only to detect, but also to home in on and destroy radar-emitting targets.

Radars can also be fooled by using deception. The very simple device known as 'chaff' or 'window' was used during World War II and is still effective in producing a radar 'smoke-screen' or decoying missiles with a deceptive cloud of radar-reflecting, metal-foil strips, aluminized nylon or glassfibre threads, etc. In theory, an aircraft which was being chased by a radar-homing missile, could throw its pursuer off the scent by releasing a small cloud of chaff. However, the subtlest forms of deception are electronic.

ECM pods, such as the Marconi Skyshadow mentioned earlier can jam in either of two modes. The first is straightforward noise

51 The Grumman EF-111A Raven developed from the F-111 fighter-bomber is used for tactical jamming of hostile radars and communications. Receiver aerials are mounted on top of the fin and transmitter aerials are located in the under-fuselage pod. (*Photograph courtesy Grumman*)

52 The RAF Jaguar's ability to deliver bombs accurately owes much to the LRMTS fitted behind the small glass windows in the chisel-nose. (*Photograph courtesy British Aerospace*)

jamming, the second is deception. In this second mode the pod mimics the radar's pulse characteristics and scanning rate so accurately that it covers the screen with hundreds of false targets, making it difficult to locate the precise source of the jamming.

If one could devise some way of making an aircraft totally invisible to radar, one would never need to work again. Sadly, total invisibility or some kind of 'anti-radar' is unlikely ever to be achieved, but it is possible to design future tactical aircraft in such a way that their radar image is greatly reduced. Radar-absorbing materials can be used for the aircraft's skin, and other parts of the structure can be designed in such a way that they *deflect* the radar energy off at an angle rather than *reflect* it straight back at the receiver.

LASERS

Lasing techniques can produce coherent radiation at or near the wavelengths of visible light. This radiation can be focussed into very narrow beams which have a number of applications, for example, accurate rangefinding. A laser pulse can be directed at quite a small target and the time taken for its return can be measured. This is the system used to achieve very accurate bomb-aiming in a number of ground-attack military aircraft, such as the RAF's Jaguars, Harrier GR.3s and the Russian MiG-27 *Flogger*.

Another application of lasers is for target marking. A soldier on the ground aims a laser designator at a target and calls in an air strike with Laser-Guided Glide Bombs (LGBs). A seeker head and steering mechanism attached to the nose of the bomb cause it to home in on the reflected laser energy, and a direct hit is almost certain.

Current military lasers are of the Neodymium type, emitting infra-red radiation at a wavelength of 1.06 microns. Although such 'light' is invisible, it is very close to the red end of the visible spectrum, and can be focussed by the lens of the eye, causing blindness. Newer CO_2 lasers operate in the mid infra-red at 10.6 microns and are eye-safe by comparison, but very few of these lasers have as yet been deployed. Another difficulty with lasers is that they work best in clear weather and are less than successful in conditions of heavy haze, mist or battlefield dust and smoke.

PASSIVE ELECTROMAGNETIC SYSTEMS

All the systems mentioned so far have been active ones, in that it is necessary for the aircraft, radar station or laser designator to transmit or emit energy in some form which could give away its position to an enemy. Passive systems, on the other hand, are those which emit no energy at all, but are designed to locate targets by means of the small amounts of heat or light the targets themselves emit. Heat-seeking missiles are well-known. They are ideal against aircraft at short ranges, homing in on the considerable amount of infra-red heat energy radiated by jet exhausts.

Other military infra-red systems use imaging techniques, building up a 'heat picture', either on photographic paper as a record, or in 'real time' on a TV screen, as with Flir (Forward-Looking Infra-red) systems. An array of very heat-sensitive semi-conductor elements cooled to 77°K is scanned to produce a picture which will reveal heat sources, such as vehicles, buildings, people etc., even at night or through fog or haze.

Just as small amounts of heat can be used to produce a picture, so can small amounts of light. TV image-intensification techniques are now so far advanced that it is possible to produce a recognizable picture using no more illumination than that produced by faint starlight. 1990s fighter aircraft will be equipped with a Visual Augmentation System (VAS) which will enable the pilot to identify targets at very long range in daylight through a stabilized telephoto lens linked to a TV screen, and at medium range using image-intensification in overcast starlight conditions, in other words, the blackest of winter's nights!

Systems employing lasers, infra-red and Low-Light Television (LLTV) usually serve the same purpose of helping the pilot to find, identify and aim at targets which would otherwise be invisible. It makes sense, therefore, to combine these Electro-Optical (EO) devices into integrated systems wherever possible. Those EO systems which are in service in front-line aircraft or recently ordered into quantity production include the following examples.

53 RF-4C reconnaissance Phantom of the US Air Force outside its hardened shelter at Zweibrücken air base, Germany

The Ferranti Laser Ranger and Marked Target Seeker (LRMTS) is standard on RAF Jaguars, Harriers and the Tornado IDS. The new French Mirage 2000, ordered for l'Armée de l'Air, will have the combined TV/laser ATLIS II pod (Autopointeur Télévision á Laser Illuminant le Sol), while the Aeronavale will equip its Atlantique patrol aircraft with a chin-mounted FLIR system. US Air Force aircraft can designate targets from the air using the Ford Aerospace Pave Tack pod which combines a FLIR and a laser designator. New American systems ordered into production include the TADS/PNVS (Target Acqusition and Designation System/Pilot Night Vision System) for the AH-64 Apache attack helicopter, combining TV, FLIR and laser systems in one package, and a system intended for fast jets called LANTIRN (Low-Altitude Navigation Targeting Infra-Red for Night) which dispenses with the need to switch on the radar.

MULTI-SENSOR RECONNAISSANCE

Knowledge is one form of power which no air force can afford to neglect. Reconnaissance can be carried out using self-contained recce pods fitted to ordinary tactical aircraft, or, alternatively, by purchasing a specially designed or adapted reconnaissance aircraft, such as the Lockheed TR-1, SR-71 Blackbird, the MiG-25E, the McDonnell-Douglas RF-4 Phantom II or the Northrop RF-5E Tiger II. Whichever reconnaissance vehicle or bolt-on pod is chosen, a number of sensor systems will be used to gather intelligence.

The US Air Force operates the RF-4C version of the Phantom in the reconnaissance role, with squadrons based at Zweibrücken in Germany and Alconbury in the UK. These Phantoms are unarmed, but their long and somewhat oddly-shaped noses contain several cameras peeping through flat glass windows, capable of forward oblique, side oblique, vertical and panoramic cross-track photography, plus infra-red line-scan for use at night or through cloud, and a choice of either passive or active radar reconnaissance systems. The Pave Tack FLIR/laser pod can also be carried.

The passive radar system is known as TEREC (Tactical Electronic Reconnaissance) and is used for pinpointing radio and radar transmitters. The active system is the SLAR (*see p. 58*) in which an antenna fitted along the lower fuselage nose just below the pilot's cockpit scans as the

54 Note windows for 'right oblique' camera at side of nose and positions of other camera windows. SLAR antenna is housed behind plain panel in lower fuselage side.

aircraft flies and builds up a surprisingly detailed radar picture of a swath of terrain out to about 10 miles (16km) to one side of the aircraft.

The resulting SLAR image looks like an aerial photograph taken from above but illuminated from one side (*see Fig. 55*). Clearly, this makes 'stand-off' reconnaissance possible, overcoming the danger of having to fly directly overhead a possibly hostile target. But there are further benefits. Near real-time reconnaissance is possible because there is no need to wait for an RF-4C to return from a mission before unloading the cameras or radar tape recorders, developing the films, processing and interpreting the results, etc. Data can be passed direct to a ground station using a directional microwave link which tracks the aircraft if it is within line of sight. Thus the radar, infra-red or TEREC picture can be built up at the ground station while the aircraft flies. The ground station is, moreover, mobile and air-transportable to wherever it is meant to operate.

Also based at Alconbury in the tactical reconnaissance role alongside the RF-4Cs is a squadron of Lockheed TR-1s. It is probably difficult for a layman to appreciate what this odd and unique aeroplane is all about, but perhaps nothing epitomizes the 'black box' aspects of military flying more than the TR-1, the long-winged black bird of the electromagnetic skies over Europe.

The Lockheed TR-1 is a development of the earlier and smaller U-2 spyplane which could climb to well over 70,000ft (about 21,000m) with the aid of its large wings and lightweight construction. In some ways the U-2 was a pilot's nightmare. Trying to turn it at maximum altitude caused the outer wing to enter Mach buffet while the inner wing began to enter stall buffet due to the extremely thin air, and even though the U-2 looked like an overgrown glider, it was difficult to land because it refused to sink fast enough when empty of fuel. The TR-1 is bigger, can carry more equipment, has redesigned wings for better performance at altitude and spoiler airbrakes to help it settle on to the runway when landing.

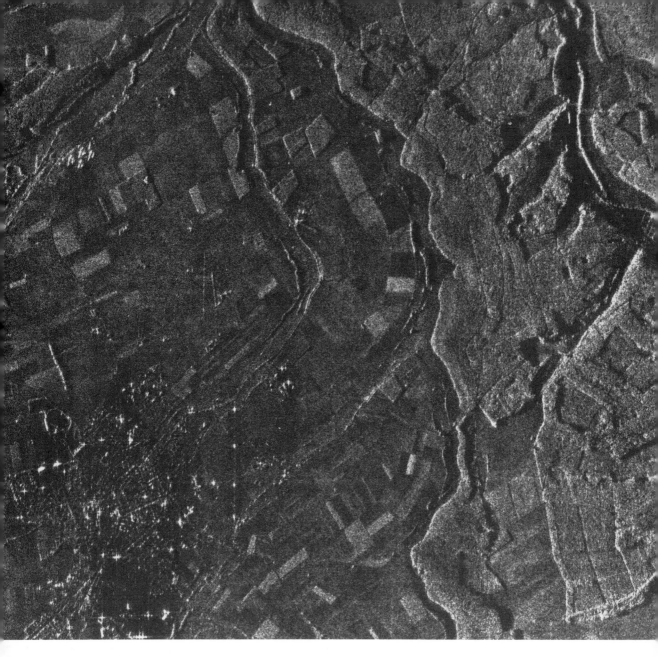

55 SLAR image of a swath of terrain approximately 10 miles (16km) wide, giving the effect of a strongly side-lit aerial photograph and is obtainable in all weathers. (*Photograph courtesy US Air Force*)

From 70,000ft (about 21,000m) or more the TR-1s from Alconbury can keep a watchful eye on what is happening in Eastern Europe in peace or war. Very few details are available on the equipment carried either in the nose or the long wing pods, but these are bolt-on units, interchangeable in a matter of minutes for other similar-looking pods containing different active or passive sensors according to the requirements of the mission.

Active systems which can be bolted on probably include SLAR similar to that carried by the RF-4, and ASARS (Advanced Synthetic Aperture Radar System) capable of producing radar maps detailed enough to pick out moving armour when compared with a reference map. Passive systems probably include a version of TEREC known as PELS (Precision Emitter Location System) capable of pinpointing individual transmitters, including jammers, by triangulation from several TR-1s if necessary. As the TR-1

56 Pictures by heat. The British Aerospace Dynamics LINESCAN 214 infra-red reconnaissance system paints pictures using the heat given off by ground installations, tanks, etc., even at night. Shown here is a test system installed in a BAe 748 Coastguarder. (*Photograph courtesy British Aerospace*)

has only one pilot, data needs to be downlinked via a chain of ground stations back to Alconbury for interpretation.

COMPUTING AND DATA DISTRIBUTION

Today's military aircraft make extensive use of electronics for all kinds of applications: radio and radar, passive sensors, flight control, weapons management and aiming, computing and the display of information to the pilot. Instead of merely 'bolting on' new gadgets as they are developed, it has always made sense to integrate any new developments into the remainder of the aircraft avionics, so that the various systems can 'talk' to one another and not merely to an already overworked pilot. In the

1970s the obvious way to arrange this was to link all avionics components and systems to a central computer, as is the case in the Tornado.

There are two snags with this arrangement where everything feeds into and is fed by a central computer. The first is weight. The wiring circuits are complicated and all the wires and cables, looms and harnesses are heavy. The second problem would arise as soon as one small section of this complex circuitry is damaged, say by a stray cannon shell. Vitally important systems are disabled and there is no back-up link to the computer.

The 1980s solution to this problem is to use a single data circuit consisting of a pair of twisted wires inside a metal sheath. This is connected to all the input sensors and output display and control units and, of course, to any computers. The *digital databus*, as the circuit is called, has the capacity to carry a great deal of information and gives each component in the system a very brief timeslot in which to 'talk' or 'listen'. The method used is called Time Division Multiplex-

57 A squadron of TR-1 tactical reconnaissance aircraft is based at USAF Alconbury, Cambridgeshire. (*Photograph courtesy Lockheed*)

58 Su-17 single seat ground attack aircraft of the Soviet Air Force with their pilots. (*Photograph courtesy Fotokhronika Tass*)

ing (TDM) and is analogous to the technology which allows thousands of simultaneous telephone conversations to take place in a single channel, or to allow large numbers of users access to the Jtids shared datalink. Because the digital databus is one circuit instead of many, it represents a great saving in weight compared to conventional circuitry, and some of this weight saving can be used to duplicate or triplicate the bus, providing parallel channels in the event of battle damage.

Using digital databuses (or should they be databi?) it is easy to see how one could go several stages further. Optical fibres carrying laser-generated light signals have an even greater information-handling capacity than metal wires. They are also smaller and lighter and much more resistant to the kind of permanent damage which could be caused by the massive Electromagnetic Pulse (EMP) from a nuclear explosion. Fibreoptic databus circuits could be replicated many times over and routed through different parts of the aircraft's structure to provide protection in the event of battle damage. Moreover, as glassfibre is regularly used to reinforce various plastics composites, an aircraft built of such materials could be reinforced by means of multiple strands of optical fibre, digital databuses, laminated into the plastic shell. Here the glass is doing two jobs, providing strength at the same time as relaying data.

As the capabilities of airborne systems improve, existing aircraft and systems can be upgraded as required without the need to rip out large parts of the structure in order to fit new radars, etc. This used to be necessary and was always a costly process. Improvements in software and processing can be made simply by taking out the old chips and replacing them with better ones. The guts of the radar remain essentially the same; it has just had a brain transplant.

4 The State of the Pilot's Art

Pilots dress for the job they have to do. Whereas a fast jet pilot will be clad in anti-gravity suit, flying overall, lifejacket, bonedome helmet with built-in microphone and oxygen mask, and then trussed-up like a chicken and strapped into an ejection seat, the crew of a large military aircraft, such as a C-135, VC-10 or Nimrod, can expect to fly in much the same shirtsleeved comfort as airline passengers, wearing just an overall or regulation flying uniform, plus perhaps a plug-in headset and lifejacket. Large military aircraft are, in many cases, descended from airliners and have all the advantages of pressurized cabins, moderate temperatures, low noise levels, toilets and catering, and do not have to make violent manoeuvres. Among the exceptions are tactical transport aircraft, such as the C-130 Hercules, where noise and vibration levels are high, and helicopters where it is also usual to wear a bonedome.

THE FAST JET PILOT

The fast jet pilot attends a pre-mission briefing wearing a flying overall with zipped pockets and transparent panels on each knee. Underneath the overall he will be wearing a pair of long pneumatically inflatable trousers called an anti-gravity suit. After the briefing he will collect lifejacket and bonedome and stow away his maps, charts, notes, etc. in the zip pockets of his overall or displayed behind the transparent knee panels. Climbing into the aircraft he straps himself into the seat and plugs in his personal equipment connector (oxygen, headset connections and compressed air for the anti-gravity suit).

The cockpits of airliners are pressurized to a pressure corresponding to the fairly low height of 8000ft (about 2400m) above sea level, where breathing is easy and no oxygen supply is needed. Those of fast jets, however, are pressurized to a lower pressure, equivalent to about 24,000ft (about 8800m) and the pilot has to breathe a mixture of air enriched with oxygen. If a pilot has to eject above this altitude, he will experience some discomfort at first.

But fast jet flying is uncomfortable enough. Today's tactics require that jets spend most of their time flying very fast in the turbulent air about 250ft above the ground, where the ride can be very bumpy indeed, although some jets, notably the F-111 and Tornado, give a much smoother ride than others – for example a Phantom.

The acceleration forces in quick pull-ups and tight turns can make every part of a pilot's body suddenly feel several times its normal weight. Fast jets can 'pull' anything up to 10 'g' or more, i.e. ten times the normal force of gravity. Quite apart from the difficulty of reaching for switches under these conditions, or turning one's head to look round, the blood will drain from a pilot's brain and he will undergo a 'blackout'. This is where the anti-gravity suit comes in. Above a certain level of acceleration a valve will open, inflating the channels in the suit with compressed air. The suit grips tightly around the pilot's stomach and legs and helps to prevent the blood draining from his brain, with the resutlt that he can cope with pulling up to 7 'g' or even 8 'g' without blacking out.

Even though it may be air-conditioned, the cockpit of a fast jet can be an uncomfortable, hot and sweaty place. Above the clouds, the heat from the sun streams in through the perspex canopy and the physical strain of violent manoeuvres or the bumpiness of low-level flying can leave a pilot feeling drained and almost sick by the time he lands again. But this is nothing to what he is going to feel if he decides to leave his aircraft in a hurry.

Ejecting

The best place for the ejection seat handle is where the pilot can reach it without getting himself into an awkward posture and perhaps causing compression fractures of the spine as the rockets in the seat-pack fire. Between the pilot's legs is the current favoured place for the yellow and black handle marked 'Pull to eject'. All he has to do is to reach down and pull, thereby triggering a chain of events over which he has little direct control.

Bang! The canopy shatters or is jettisoned, the seat straps and leg restraints tighten, pulling the pilot back into the seat as the main seat cartridge fires, blasting the pilot and seat out of the aircraft. A rocket motor then fires for 0.25 seconds taking the pilot well clear before a sequence of drogue parachutes are released to slow the seat down. The main parachute will not deploy until the seat has fallen to a pre-programmed altitude, say 12,000ft (about 3600m). By the time the pilot reaches this altitude he is safely dangling beneath the main parachute and the seat has fallen away.

On landing, the pilot only has his flying gear, parachute, an inflatable dinghy with cover and radio-locator beacon, a lifejacket and some rations in a Personal Survival Pack. On these he must survive, possibly in a freezing winter sea or in the mountains in bad weather, until rescued. If he 'bangs out' over enemy-held territory in wartime, he must, of course, try to evade capture.

THE PRINCIPLES OF AIRMANSHIP

Despite the computerization of cockpits and flightdecks, the basic principles of airmanship have not changed. The pilot still has to get his machine off the ground, fly it safely in what is often very crowded airspace, deal with emergencies should any arise, find his airfield and land again. Over the years, systems have been evolved to help him, such as Air Traffic Control, and it is on the shoulders of radar-equipped air traffic controllers that the main responsibility for avoiding mid-air collisions rests, particularly at night or in cloud when the pilot cannot always expect to 'see and be seen'.

From his very early days in a basic trainer, the pilot learns to fly visual circuits which consist of: take-off, climb to 1000ft (about 300m), turn on to a downwind leg, prepare to land, then fly a base-leg and final approach to the runway. The subsequent landing will either be an overshoot, a 'roller' (touch and go) or a land and stop. This circuit is practised continually and forms the basis of aircraft handling, even when the pilot has graduated to a front-line squadron. When a military aircraft returns from a long sortie, the pilot may do a practice overshoot before going round again and landing.

A formation of fast jets will habitually execute a 'run-in and break' if the weather is good enough for a visual landing. This manoeuvre consists of a fast approach to the airfield at about 1000ft (about 300m) and 400 knots (461mph). When overhead, each plane in the formation will 'break' sharply in turn to form a line astern on the downwind leg, completing the circuit and landing close behind each other.

At night or in low cloud, the approach must be flown on instruments until the runway lights can be seen dead ahead. There are several methods of doing this. In a Tornado, the ground mapping radar produces a clear enough picture of the runway for the navigator to talk the pilot down. Other aircraft may have to rely on a GCA (Ground Controlled Approach) where the pilot is talked down by a ground-based radar controller. Many airfields have a purpose-designed Precision Approach Radar (PAR), usually housed in a small church-like building close to the main runway. If the airfield has a TACAN or other radio beacon, the pilot can home in on this. However at most large airfields there will be at least one ILS (Instrument Landing System). The main antenna of an ILS looks somewhat like an electronic fence just off the far end of the runway, with additional transmitters close to the landing end of the runway and along the final approach. The sharp end of the ILS is an instrument with crossed pointers on the aircraft flight deck. The pilot flies so as to keep the pointers centralized, and this should keep him in the centre of the radio beams and take him to within sight of the runway.

Working at the sharp end of a fast jet is very demanding, particularly if there is only one pilot and no navigator, observer, weapons systems officer or other form of 'talking ballast' in the back seat. Powered controls, fly-by-wire controls, automatic pilots, computerized navi-

59 The control tower provides visual surveillance of the airfield and runways. Dutch Air Force controllers in the tower at Twenthe. (*Photograph courtesy Koninklijke Luchtmacht*)

gation and weapon-delivery systems are essential if the pilot is to get the most out of his aircraft.

Relaxed Static Stability

The main flying controls operate hydraulically in response to movements of the pilot's joystick or rudder pedals. It used to be thought necessary to feed back some element of artificial 'feel' to the joystick so that the pilot could have some idea of how the controls were responding, but, with the advent of computers, this is no longer quite so important. If we work on the assumption that it is possible to programme a computer so that it understands the plane's handling better (and can react far more quickly) than any pilot, we have what is known popularly as Fly-By-Wire and more accurately as Active Control Technology (ACT). The General Dynamics F-16 Fighting Falcon, now in service with five air forces is the first example of the Fly-By-Wire

principle exploited to take advantage of the benefits of Relaxed Static Stability (RSS), but Fly-By-Wire itself is nothing new. Essentially it consists of using motion sensors and a computer to take over at least some of the tasks of handling an aircraft and keeping it in stable flight. For years, conventional aircraft had little need of such a system because they possessed inherent stability in all three flight axes provided by a vertical fin, a varying downforce on the tail and some device, such as wing sweep or dihedral. If the pilot were to let go of the controls the aircraft would still continue in stable flight.

This was less true however, of helicopters. Helicopters are inherently less stable than fixed-wing aircraft and need to incorporate some kind of Stability Augmentation System (SAS) to make things easier for the pilot. Computers can react very quickly to changes in an aircraft's attitude and can apply corrective inputs. Fixed-wing designs, such as the Tornado began to incorporate computers into their control linkages, making a fixed-wing aircraft's inherent stability redundant. The F-16 has no inherent longitudinal stability whatever. A

60 The crew of a Tupolev Tu-28P long range interceptor; Lieutenant Colonel N. Gaidukov and Major V. Leonov check over their flightplan. (*Photograph courtesy Fotokhronika Tass*)

quadruplexed analogue computer applies the controls immediately to correct any deviation from the flight path intended by the pilot.

The pilot of an F-16 communicates with the flight control computer by means of a short 'stick' in his right hand. This joystick barely moves but is able to sense pressures from the pilot's hand requesting 'nose-up, nose-down, turn left, turn right' and the computer immediately and definitively decides whether or not a particular manoeuvre is feasible. Near the stall, for example, the computer will certainly override the pilot's command if he should try to pitch the nose further up.

The benefits of RSS can be realized in various ways. With no continual stabilizing downforce on the tail, aerodynamic efficiency is improved. Air combat manoeuvring is enhanced, as in the F-16, and the new Mirages, the 2000, 4000 and 3NG can get their delta wings to work harder,

reducing the landing and take-off speeds. British Aerospace is busy testing a quadruplex *digital* Fly-By-Wire system in a Jaguar testbed, and new, experimental versions of the F-16 are pushing the RSS technology even further forward.

The pilot of an F-16 does not sit in his seat – he reclines. The couch is angled back to 30° inside a one-piece cockpit canopy providing all-round vision. The pilot positions his forearms on padded siderests, gripping the stick with his right hand and the throttle with his left. All the controls he needs in order to fight the aircraft are in the form of finger and thumb switches, even the controls for the radar. Hands-on-Throttle-and-Stick (HOTAS) at all times when it matters; no straining against massive g-forces to fumble for a switch.

Integrated Systems and Displays

Other technological developments are also invading the fighter cockpit and have been doing so for quite some time. Systems are being integrated. In the Tornado, for example, most of

61 Photograph of F-16 cockpit taken down the sloping back of the pilot's couch showing ejection-seat handle in centre, short 'joystick' on the right and throttle lever (with thumbwheels) on left. On top of the coaming is the HUD with controls below. The radar display is in the centre, and on the left is a multifunctions display with circular screen of RWR above. (*Photograph courtesy General Dynamics*)

62 and 63 More views of the F-16 cockpit

the systems interface with the main computer: air data systems which sense speed and altitude, navigation and approach aids, radar, communications and weapons systems. All of these can talk to the main computer and through it to the various cockpit displays. The myriad agglomeration of circular dials and multiple pointers, each for its own separate instrument, which used to festoon a fighter's panel, are beginning to give way to large, square-faced CRT displays and multi-function keyboards. The 'essential and basic' instruments, such as artificial horizon, compass and altimeter, are being relegated to a standby role as the TV screens stage a takeover.

Automated systems handle much of the workload of routine flying. Automatic pilots will not only fly the aircraft straight and level, but will steer it from one waypoint to the next in accor-

64 Fly-By-Wire Jaguar testbed. (*Photograph courtesy British Aerospace*)

dance with the pre-programmed navigation flightplan. Terrain-Following Radar (TFR) linked to the autopilot makes flying a Tornado at 200ft (60m) and 600 knots (700mph) straightforward. The TFR keeps a lookout ahead for hills, trees, pylons and other hazards, and its computer decides whether to command the autopilot to pull up or go round these obstacles. Even pre-takeoff checks are partially automated in the Tornado, using a facility called BITE (*see p.27*). One might indeed wonder what is there left for the pilot and navigator to do.

Dominating the view ahead from a fighter cockpit is the HUD, or Head Up Display. This device is a latter-day development of the gyro gunsight which projected an aiming symbol on a piece of angled glass. A HUD is much larger and the image is computer-generated and projected from a TV tube. There is, theoretically, no limit to the amount of information which can

be supplied to the pilot through the HUD – altitude, speed, navigation information, weapons-aiming symbology, even radar, FLIR and LLTV imagery if required – making it unnecessary for the pilot to look down at the instrument panel during air-to-air combat or ground attack.

NAVIGATION

Although student pilots learn to navigate using map and compass, such simple methods can only be followed in broad daylight when there is very little cloud. Navigating today's aircraft is a task which relies mainly on computers or radio aids, or both. Maps and charts are still carried. They enable the pilot to recognize the target area or to find his way to an unfamiliar airfield, and in the unlikely event that sophisticated navigation systems went wrong, he would feel rather silly if he did not have a basic map.

How does an electronic system manage to navigate an aircraft and tell the pilot where he is? There are at least two parts to the answer. The first is that the navigation system must have some *inputs*, i.e. some means of knowing or of computing its present position. The second is that there must be some convenient way to display this information to the pilot so that he can interpret it in order to get his aeroplane to where he wants to go – i.e. some kind of *output*.

Ground-Based Systems

The earliest electronic navigation systems used ground-based radio beacons in conjunction with an airborne direction finder. This system, known as ADF (*see p.51*) is so basic that it is still used on many aircraft, and the landscape is dotted with large numbers of simple radio beacons operating in the LF/MF bands; small huts containing a low-power transmitter with tall poles outside.

Networks of more sophisticated beacon systems now exist, such as the civil aviation VOR/DME system working in the VHF/UHF bands, and its Western military counterpart TACAN (Tactical Aerial Navigation), which is a network of UHF beacons each of which occupies one of 252 channels in the 962 – 1215 MHz band. Important military airfields have their own TACAN beacon, which looks like a large dustbin mounted on a platform, and TACANs are also installed in a few other sites (*see Fig.66*). A TACAN provides the pilot of a suitably equipped aircraft with a read-out of bearing and distance to the beacon, usually displayed on the compass instrument, and the system is best used for homing; TACAN is accurate to within 1° of bearing and one-fifth of a nautical mile in distance. The main disadvantage with TACAN as a military system is that it would be very vulnerable in wartime, as would all ground-based installations.

Loran, *Decca* and *Omega* are long-range systems which broadcast synchronized signals from pairs of transmitters. Receiving equipment aboard the aircraft measures any small time-difference between the signals, producing a display which can be resolved into a position line on a chart. By tuning other stations in the chain, more position lines can be derived, and where these intersect on the chart is the aircraft's position. The only one of these three systems which looks like having an assured

65 A TACAN beacon

future is *Omega*. By using a unique method of transmitting their signals, the entire globe can be covered by no more than eight Omega stations, owned and maintained by the US Navy, and operating on VLF frequencies. Omega receivers fitted aboard aircraft are small black boxes which take up very little space and are easily installed. They compute the aircraft's position as coordinates of latitude and longitude on LED displays and, if necessary, can be interfaced with an autopilot.

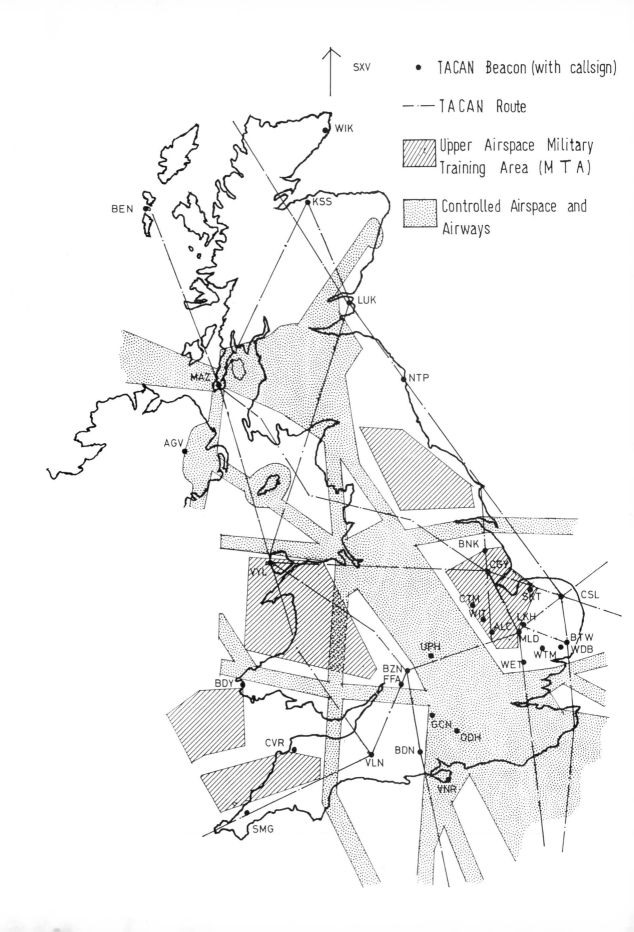

SXV

• TACAN Beacon (with callsign)

–·– TACAN Route

Upper Airspace Military Training Area (MTA)

Controlled Airspace and Airways

WIK

BEN

KSS

LUK

NTP

MAZ

AGV

VYL

BNK

CRY

CTM · SXT · CSL

WTI · LKH

ALC

MLD · BTW

WTM · WDB

WET

UPH

BZN
FFA

BDY

GCN · ODH

CVR

VLN · BDN

VNR

SMG

66 TACAN beacons and associated military airspace arrangements

67 Doppler navigation computer and display. (*Photograph courtesy Marconi Avionics Limited*)

Navstar Satellites

Navstar has the doubtful advantage that the reference stations are orbiting in space about 12,000 miles (20,000km) away, and unless Space Wars technology improves they are safe, at least for the time being. A network of up to 18 or more Navstar satellites would be needed for full global coverage and the system would work as follows. Each satellite transmits its present position and a very accurate time signal. These are picked up by a receiver on the ground, or in an aircraft, and the time reference signal would in each case be around 0.06 seconds late, because of the distance. Distances to and positions of at least three Navstar satellites would be triangulated in the receiver's computer to give a very accurate position read-out.

Self-Contained Airborne Navigation Systems

Navigation systems which are completely self-contained within the aircraft, needing no external point of reference such as a beacon, transmitter chain or satellites would be the safest to use in wartime. Such systems are *Doppler*, *INS* and *Lasernav*.

Doppler

Doppler is the older and simplest of these but is supposedly the least accurate. Doppler is a continuous-wave radio or radar system which beams signals at the ground (or sea) and measures the Doppler shift in the frequency of the returned signals to obtain an accurate estimate of the aircraft's forward speed. The principle is exactly the same as that used by the local police to check the speed of road vehicles. Doppler beams also measure *drift*, i.e. speed sideways, resulting from crosswinds of which the pilot may not be aware. Early Doppler displays simply told the pilot or the navigator the aircraft's speed and drift. He then used his charts, rulers, protractors and stopwatch to work out his present position from his last known position. State-of-the-art Doppler systems have built in microprocessors which compute and display the aircraft's present position continuously.

Inertial Navigation Systems (INS)

INS (Inertial Navigation Systems) use accelerometers mounted on gyro-stabilized platforms to measure acceleration in three axes. Acceleration can be computed to give speed and this can be computed to give distance, which can, in turn, be computed to give position. As with Doppler, provided that the computer has been told the aircraft's starting position at the beginning of the flight, it can display this position continuously as latitude and longitude using LEDs.

Lasernav

Lasernav is beginning to replace INS in many aircraft, as it has no mechanical moving parts such as gyros, gimbals, etc. which can go wrong. A beam of laser light is generated inside a triangular transparent medium, either glass or some suitable gas at low pressure. The laser beam is sent *both ways* round this triangular block and is reflected by mirrors at the corners. If the block remains stationary the light waves will arrive in phase; if the block moves, the light waves will arrive at the output sensor out-of-phase and will set up an interference phenomenon which can be sensed and measured.

Such a system fitted in an aircraft will measure speed, and this can be used to compute the aircraft's position. Laser navigation systems are compact and accurate. Unlike the INS they are bolted directly into the aircraft (a *strapdown* system) and do not need to be suspended in carefully engineered gimbals, bearings, etc. Another advantage is that, unlike gyros, it does not need several minutes to spin up to working speed. A laser is ready for use almost as soon as it is switched on, and it is for this reason that the Honeywell Laser Navigation System was chosen for Northrop's F-20 Tigershark. This has an 'alignment time' of only 22 seconds, making it possible to 'scramble' the Tigershark very quickly if required.

Integrated Navigation and Weapons Systems

There are now available several different types of navigation systems, of varying degrees of accuracy and reliability, and fitting into black boxes of varying sizes, all of which can compute the aircraft's position in latitude and longitude and display this to the pilot. However, the pilot of a tactical aircraft has no time to be fiddling with maps and scaling off latitude and longitude read-outs in order to keep track of his progress. The navigation system must provide more help to the pilot, either by being able to interface with the autopilot, the radar, a moving map display or a combination of all three.

A navigation computer should be able to interface with the autopilot in such a way that it can steer the aircraft to each one of a set of waypoints in turn, chosen at the flight-planning stage and programmed into the navigation system's computer. This is what the NAVWASS (Navigation and Weapon-Aiming Sub-System) fitted to the RAF's Jaguars is able to do. At the heart of NAVWASS is Ferranti FIN 1064 inertial navigation system which is so precise that it can, if necessary, be used to steer a Jaguar all the way to its target and release the weapons without the pilot ever having seen very much – the so-called 'blind first-pass attack'. However, to be certain the navigation system remains accurate throughout the flight, it can be updated by reference to any visual features likely to be spotted by the pilot, for example a conspicuous bridge which has already been programmed as a waypoint into the computer. As the Jaguar approaches the bridge, a symbol will appear on

68 Lasernav: this model illustrates the compactness of the system. (*Photograph courtesy British Aerospace Dynamics*)

69 The Northrop F-20 Tigershark is a new fighter intended mainly for export and is the first new fighter to be equipped with a Lasernav. (*Photograph courtesy Northrop*)

70 Tornado GR.1 from 9 Squadron, RAF Honington, Suffolk on a training sortie over Fylingdales Moor in North York- shire with the 'golf ball' radomes of the Early Warning Station clearly visible. (*Photograph courtesy T.R. Paxton*)

the pilot's HUD telling him where the computer thinks the bridge is. If this is not quite correct, the pilot can use his hand controller to re- position the waypoint symbol exactly on top of the bridge, then punch a button with his thumb. The NAVWASS is now accurately updated and, provided the INS remains accurate and does not wander, the system will steer the pilot to his target as planned.

There is, however, a further refinement. Maps are useful to a pilot, but fumbling with maps in the cockpit during a low-level tactical mission is not really feasible. The Jaguar uses an optically projected moving map display which is slaved to the NAVWASS. Maps likely to be needed are photographed onto 35mm film and stored in the aircraft for projection on to a large circular screen which dominates the centre of the Jaguar's instrument panel. The display moves to keep pace with the Jaguar's passage over the ground.

Unlike Jaguars, the IDS Tornado has ground- mapping radar, and this can be used to update the navigation system, provided that a radar- significant waypoint can be clearly identified. Again, bridges are favourites, but electricity pylons, tall chimneys and large buildings will also show clearly on radar. Tornado's ability to use its ground-mapping radar makes it ideally suited to night and bad weather missions. The radar display is in the rear cockpit of the IDS Tornado and is monitored by the navigator, sharing a screen with the moving-map display with which it should coincide. The pilot also has a CRT screen with a repeat of the moving-map without the radar display. Ferranti, who de- signed the video-projected moving-map dis- play for the Tornado has further developed this into an off-the-shelf system called COMED (Combined Map and Electronic Display) which is being fitted to the F/A-18 Hornet fighter and the Indian Air Force's Jaguars. In France, Thomson CSF have developed a similar dis- play called MERCATOR (Map Electronic Re- mote Colour Autonomous Television Output Reader), which will be fitted in the Mirage 2000.

71 Cockpit of RAF Jaguar showing the large circular screen for the projected moving map display, to its left the main flight instruments and above this the keypad and LED displays of the FIN 1064 inertial navigation system controller. At the lower left is a hand-controller which allows a HUD symbol to be moved in order to update the navigation system. (*Photograph courtesy British Aerospace*)

NAVIGATION SYSTEMS IN ACTION

Thus, the pilot or navigator of a ground-attack aircraft prepares for a mission by punching the latitude and longitude coordinates of way-points, radar-significant points, visually significant points and those of the target into the keypad of his navigation computer. If his aircrft is a single-seater, such as a Jaguar or Harrier, this adds significantly to the pilot's workload just prior to take-off. Even if there is a backseater to do all this, mistakes can still arise due to 'finger-trouble'. With the IDS Tornado, the entire flightplan can be prepared beforehand, using computers and plotting tables, then stored in a standard C-60 tape cassette. Once on board the aircraft, the navigator inserts the

72 COMED 2036 in the moving map mode. (*Photograph courtesy Ferranti*)

cassette into the CVR (Cockpit Voice Recorder) which programmes the flightplan into the navigation system.

It is because ground-attack aircraft such as Tornado must be able to attack unseen targets accurately that they need very precise navigation systems. Tornado's navigation computer accepts both INS and Doppler inputs, then uses a statistical technique, called Kalman filtering, to decide which is likely to be most accurate. The result is that a Tornado can navigate accurately to within less than one nautical mile per hour of flying time. In other words, after an hour's treetop flying dodging around hostile radar and missile sites at 600 knots (about 700mph), a Tornado will still be less than a mile away from where it thinks it is. In practice, the errors will be much less than this because the crew will update the navigation frequently, using fixes taken from visual or radar-significant features of the landscape. The exact positions of the target and of waypoint fixes en route will be known from accurately surveyed maps compiled from satellite photographs or by using reconnaissance aircraft.

A typical Tornado mission might be to plant a 1000lb (450kg) bomb on top of a command bunker. This is known to be a certain bearing and distance from an electricity pylon. The pylon will show up on radar and can be used to update the navigation system precisely, after which the Tornado will find and bomb the bunker automatically.

5 The Mind of a Missile

CARRYING WEAPONS

In the training of every fast jet pilot the day comes when he takes off carrying live weapons for the first time. His first task, and also that of every trainee armourer, is to learn to handle these weapons safely. Weapons ought not to explode if they are dropped accidentally on to the tarmac while being loaded onto an aircraft, if they fall off accidentally in flight, or are jetti- soned in an emergency. They are prevented from exploding by a number of separate elec- trical and mechanical arming devices, and need to be armed before being used with hostile intent.

Only a small number of aircraft (e.g. the Buccaneer and the F-111) carry weapons in

73 Fitting a Harpoon anti-ship missile to the underwing pylon of a Lockheed P-3 Orion. (*Photograph courtesy McDonnell-Douglas*)

74 The missile at the moment of release, the attachment lugs and screwpads show clearly. (*Photograph courtesy McDonnell-Douglas*)

internal bomb bays. The vast majority carry their weapons, apart from guns, on wing or fuselage pylons. Pylons can be fitted to or removed from underwing hardpoints in a short time, and almost all pylons are standard, capable of carrying anything which can be fitted with a pair of NATO standard lugs, spaced 14in. apart, plus appropriate electrical, mechanical or fuel connections. Examples of stores which fit directly to pylons include fuel tanks, bombs, rocket packs, ECM pods, and certain missiles. Adapters containing launch rails for missiles such as Sidewinders also fit directly to pylons.

When a bomb is offered up to a pylon, hooks grip the lugs on the bomb and hold it safely. Screwpads are tightened onto the curvature of the bomb to prevent it swaying from side to side and the electrical and mechanical arming and fusing connections are completed. The bomb is still safe. As the aircraft heads for the runway the pilot will operate the Master Arm switch and check that the correct arming and fusing logic has been programmed into the Weapons Management System. Nearer the target he selects the pylons he wishes to use and arms and fuses each weapon. If he omits any of these procedures the bomb will not be released at all, or, if it is, it will fall 'safe', i.e. unarmed, and fail to explode.

The release sequence is triggered electric-

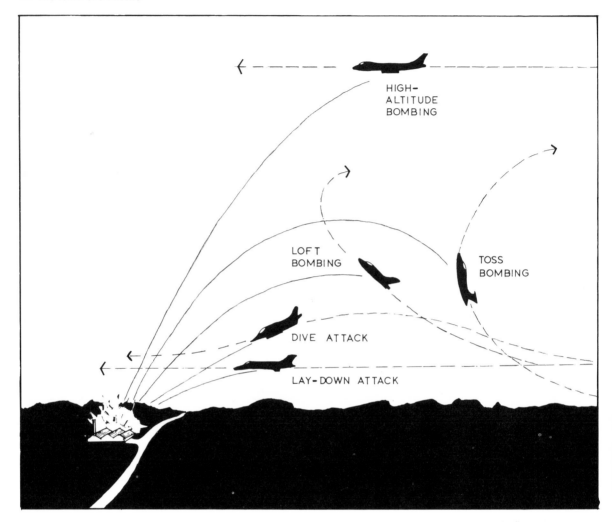

75 Ground-attack techniques

ally, usually from a button on the pilot's joystick or in response to computer-generated release timing. The electrical signal fires a pair of explosive cartridges in the pylon ERU (Explosive Release Unit) generating a charge of high-pressure gas. This forces apart the hooks holding the lugs on the bomb and operates a pushrod to assist gravity in getting the bomb safely clear of the pylon. As the bomb falls away it is still attached by means of a thin wire static line. If this static line comes away easily, the bomb will fall 'safe'. Should the bomb be armed, an electromagnetic lock will detain the loop on the static line, causing the bomb to use most of its weight to pull itself free. The end of the line

attached to the bomb can now 'snatch' heavily enough to start the arming sequence, which includes opening the drogue parachute on a retarded bomb.

Long-range fuel tanks are carried on pylons in the same way as bombs. They are connected to a self-sealing fuel line and compressed air is used to force the fuel out of the tanks. During combat, empty tanks can be jettisoned using the ERU in the same way as if they were bombs. In an emergency, say following an engine failure after take-off, the pilot can clear all the pylons by using a single 'clear pylons' switch to activate all ERUs. Tanks would fall clear and bombs would fall safe.

Learning to Bomb

Seeing a target is one thing; hitting it accurately with gunfire, rocket projectiles or bombs is another matter. Ground targets are attacked in a dive when using guns or rockets. Low-level bombing is best done from a flat ('lay down') approach, and computerized modes are available for 'loft' and 'toss' bombing. The student pilot may graduate later in his career to aircraft with sophisticated weapon-aiming systems such as the Jaguar, Harrier, F-111, A-6 or Tornado, but while still a student he practises the difficult art of delivering weapons by eye. In the case of an RAF pilot he will learn this exacting skill while flying Hawks of the Tactical Weapons Units (TWU) at Brawdy or Chivenor.

The Hawks at Brawdy and Chivenor are essentially the same as those with which the student fast jet pilot will be familiar from his days at RAF Valley, but the pylons can carry containers for 6½lb (3kg) practice bombs, rocket projectiles and a centreline, mounted 20mm Aden cannon. The cockpit has the arming switches for all of this dangerous equipment, an ISIS (Integrated Sight and Interception System) combination bombsight and air-to-air gyro gunsight, plus a gunsight camera to check how well the pilot has aimed the aircraft when he 'presses the button'.

The ISIS sight is smaller than a latter-day HUD and does not have all the complicated symbology, but it does project on the angled reflector glass a 'budgie' symbol to indicate the aircraft's flightpath, an inverted 'T' symbol for the gun boresight, and an aiming mark or 'pipper' surrounded by a circle. This can be deflected or depressed on relation to the other two marks to take account of range, wind, crosswind, ballistic properties of different weapons, dive angle and air-to-air lead. The optics in the reflector gunsight focus all these marks on infinity and they can be aimed accurately independently of the position of the pilot's head.

BALLISTICS

Ballistics is the science and art of throwing or firing a weapon so that the missile or projectile hits its target. Bullets, rocket projectiles and bombs are all subject to the force of gravity from

76 ISIS bombsight camera photograph of a simulated attack on a Bloodhound surface-to-air missile site, showing the aiming pipper of the sight in the centre of the illuminating radar. The inverted 'T' indicating the aircraft's boresight is visible just below the horizon. (*Photograph courtesy RAF*)

the moment of their release until they make impact. They will also be affected by the wind. A gun must be aimed high and into any wind that happens to be blowing and, in practice, what a pilot has to do is to programme the aiming 'pipper' of his ISIS to take account of these deflections. From printed tables the pilot can check how many 'mills' he must depress or slew the pipper off the boresight for a particular type of attack.

To fire the gun the arming switches must be set and the correct aiming depression selected in 'mills' to take account of the range and dive angle. The gun (and the ISIS camera) is operated by means of a guarded trigger on the joystick. If rocket projectiles are carried, these can be selected to fire either singly or in a staggered salvo known as a 'ripple'. If they were all fired at once they would interfere with each other in flight. Similarly, when bombs are released there is always a small time delay between the release of bombs on adjacent pylons.

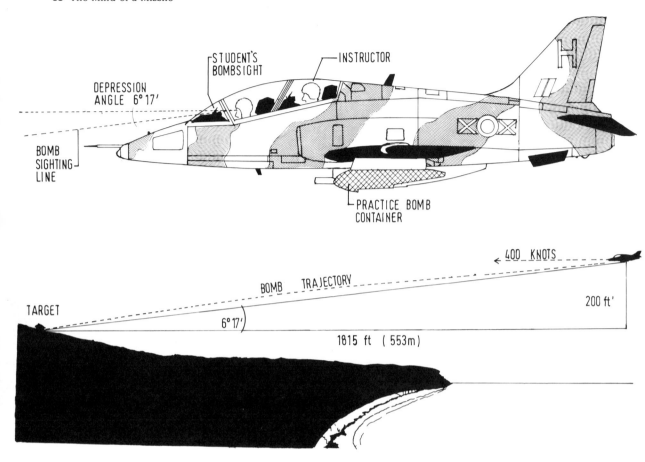

77 The geometry of a lay-down bombing run

A typical 'lay-down' bombing run would consist of a flat approach to the target at a pre-selected height and speed. If 400 knots (460mph) at 200ft were selected, then it is known that a typical low-drag bomb would travel 1815ft between release and impact. Solve this triangle and you get a depression angle of just over 6°17'. From tables the pilot will be able to set up the correct number of 'mills' on the aiming pipper to correspond with this angle and to offset the pipper to allow for any crosswind. His task now is to approach the target at the exact speed of 400 knots and as close as possible to dead level at 200ft. Select pylon and store. Complete arming. As the target comes into view, fly straight towards it, level, at the correct height and speed. When the flap on the joystick guarding the release button is opened the camera will start rolling and the aiming pipper will depress to the pre-set angle. At the split second when the target and pipper coincide, the button is pressed and the bombs released.

Air-to-Air Gunnery

The other function of the ISIS sight is in air-to-air gunnery. This is no problem if you sneak up on your quarry from his 'six o'clock' and he hasn't seen you. As soon as he does see you he will 'break' violently away and you will be forced to follow him round the turn. To aim at him at all you need to turn more tightly than he does and to aim *ahead* to compensate for the distance he will travel before the cannon shells reach him. This is known as 'lead' and the aiming pipper of the gyro gunsight estimates this lead for you by assuming that you and your quarry are carrying out similar manoeuvres. As you twist and turn, the gyro in the gunsight drives the pipper up and down and from side to side. When you manage to get the pipper lined up with your quarry, you fire (*see Fig. 121, 1a–c*).

This kind of technology is used in training fast jet pilots to shoot and bomb accurately, but it is not particularly new and, in practice, it would not be at all accurate. Present-day weapon-aiming technology tries to ensure that every bomb, rocket, missile and cannon shell finds its target, and varying degrees of accuracy are possible depending on the system used.

Helicopter Weaponry

The Bell AH-1 Cobra helicopter gunship emerged in Vietnam and has undergone considerable improvement since. US Army AH-1S Cobra units based in Europe expect that, if they are ever shooting in anger again, their target will be heavily armoured tanks and not just Vietnamese peasants running for cover. The Cobra is armed with rockets, TOW missiles and a three-barrelled 20mm gun. The rockets are fired by the pilot from the back seat using a HUD which is not unlike the ISIS gunsight described above. The rocket launch tubes are fixed, so it is necessary for the pilot to aim the helicopter accurately, using a laser rangefinder to obtain an accurate read-out of range, while estimates of windspeed are provided by a Low Airspeed Indicator mounted on a boom to one side of the cockpit. The rockets have a range of about 4 miles (more than 6km) and can be fitted with a variety of warheads. They can be fired singly, in pre-set groups or in a ripple.

In the Cobra's front seat is a gunner whose chief toy is a gyro-stabilized Telescopic Sighting Unit (TSU) mounted in a chin-turret. This is a telescope which can be used to line up distant targets on the crosshairs, then 'caged' so that it will continue 'looking' at the target whatever the antics of the helicopter. Ranging information from the laser, plus wind data, are fed to the fire control computer which lines up the gun. Accuracy is guaranteed. If a TOW missile is selected and fired, an infra-red source on the rear of the missile is tracked and used to line up the missile's flight with the crosshairs of the TSU. Steering commands to the missile are passed

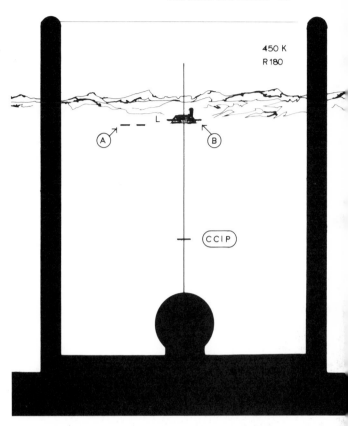

78 Simplified representation of the view through a Jaguar HUD during a bombing run. The labels in arrowed circles do not appear on the real HUD and are merely explanatory, while the circular shape at the bottom is the silhouette of the HUD camera. The speed (450 knots [518mph]) derived from the navigation system and the height (180ft [55m]) derived from the radar altimeter are shown in the top right-hand corner. The vertical line up the middle of the display is the Bomb Fall Line and the mark on this is the CCIP which shows where on the terrain the bombs would fall if they were to be released *now*. The navigation computer has indicated where it thinks the target is at 'A' by means of a broken horizontal line which the pilot has moved using his hand controller to the actual target, the building at 'B'. The marker will remain stabilized on the building as the Jaguar flies towards it and the symbol 'L' shows that the pilot has fired the laser ranger to check the exact range. The target marker will remain superimposed on the target and both will move down the Bomb Fall Line until they reach the CCIP at which point the bombs will be released automatically.

along a thin wire which unreels as the missile flies, carrying its shaped-charge warhead to penetrate the tank's armour. As long as the gunner keeps the crosshairs centred on the tank, the latter's fate is sealed.

Helmet-Pointing

Helmet-pointing is another recent development which allows helicopter pilots and gunners to acquire their targets more quickly. The movements of the TSU or the gun can be 'slaved' to the movements of a specially fitted pilot's helmet. The sighting system then points to wherever the pilot is looking. Helicopters can launch ordnance at targets while they themselves hover stationary, or almost so, partially hidden behind trees or other cover.

Computer-Assisted Bombing Systems

By way of contrast, it is much more difficult to deliver ordnance from a fast jet travelling at anything up to 600 knots (700mph). One solution is to bomb 'blind', with the aid of computers, a target which is already programmed into the navigational system, but it is better if the pilot can *see* the target. He can then make any necessary last-second adjustments to ensure accuracy.

A number of computer-assisted bombing systems have been devised. These use the accurate inputs possible with Doppler or INS navigation, plus an accurate height read-out from a radar altimeter to 'track' a target designated by the pilot using a movable marker on his HUD. Other useful aiming information is provided by the angular speed at which the designated target moves down the HUD. A computer selects the exact moment at which to release the weapons, removing the delay inherent in the speed of reaction of the pilot's thumb. In this way the HUD, which interfaces with the Jaguar's NAVWASS (*see p.78*), continuously computes an impact point where the bombs, if released *now*, would fall. The pilot can use the displayed CCIP (Continuously Computed Impact Point) as though it were the ordinary aiming pipper of an ISIS sight, but to get the full benefit from the system, he will designate the required target on the HUD (by correcting if necessary the positioning of the navigation-computed target symbol and moving this to the actual target), and fire the laser, combined with the target's depression angle, enables the computer continuously to solve the bomb-laying triangle and predict the impact point more accurately. When the CCIP and the target marker coincide, the bombs are released automatically and should not fail to hit their targets. The NAVWASS computer can be programmed with the ballistic characteristics of a wide range of weapons, guns, rockets, low-drag bombs of various types, drogue-retarded bombs, etc.

Laser Bombing

Even when using conventional bombs greater accuracy is possible if some means can be found of marking the target with a laser.

A soldier on the ground can aim a laser designator at the target and the reflected laser light can activate the seeker head of the Jaguar or Harrier's LRMTS (*see p.62*) which will then aim its bombs at this precisely marked target. Even more accuracy is possible if the bombs are laser-guided and can steer themselves towards the target by homing in on the reflected laser light. LGBs (*see p.61*) have small wings, and, provided they are released somewhere near the target, can home in on it. Paveway LGBs, toss-bombed from RAF Harrier GR.3s, were used to good effect in the closing stages of the Falklands War.

Targets can also be designated from the air. In the Franco-American ATLIS II system (*see p.62*) which will be fitted to the French Air Force's Mirage 2000s and Jaguars, a pilot can pick out a distant target using an electro-optical TV system, which will work on poor light, and stabilize the ATLIS pod on it. This continues to point at the target, regardless of the aircraft's manoeuvres, while a laser beam is fired down the centre of the display. A laser-guided weapon can now be released at the target, either a glide bomb with an EBLIS laser tracker mounted in the nose, or, for longer, stand-off ranges, an Aerospatiale AS-30 laser-guided missile.

BOMBS FOR SPECIAL PURPOSES

Servicemen sometimes speak disparagingly of 'iron bombs', 'dumb bombs' or even 'steam bombs' and give the impression that 'smart' bombs are the answer to a whole range of military problems. Smart bombs are those which can be relied upon invariably to find their targets, and the truth about the present state-of-the-art is that some bombs are smarter than

79 Ripple-firing of rocket projectiles from a Mirage F.1. (*Photograph courtesy Matra*)

others. New, increasingly 'smart' emerging-technology (ET) weapons systems are continually being suggested, but often, when these are deployed after many years of experiment and development, they are found to 'possess operational difficulties'. In other words, they don't always work very well.

Today's RAF has two rather special requirements. The first is for a reliable method of destroying enemy armour (i.e. tanks), and the second is for a good anti-airfield weapon.

During a battle, the task of destroying tanks would be delegated primarily to helicopters in the battle area itself (*see p.89*), but deep penetration air strikes would be needed to stop enemy reinforcements getting through. A number of sophisticated stand-off weapons have been suggested for tackling these 'second echelon' armoured reinforcements, but none of these is in place as yet, and it would be left to RAF Tornadoes, armed with cluster bombs, to do what damage they could.

Cluster Bombs

Tornadoes can 'lob' cluster bombs a long way in a 'loft' or 'toss' attack. The plane climbs at a steady angle for a loft attack, or pulls up into a loop for a toss attack, while a computer works out the correct moment to release the bombs. The plane turns for home as the bombs travel in a high arc towards their target. The system can hardly be expected to be very accurate, but this is compensated for to some extent by the 'shotgun effect' of scattering the clusters of bomblets over a fairly wide area.

A single 1000lb (454kg) bomb needs to score an almost direct hit to do any significant military damage to anything other than a soft target. If it misses it digs a large hole and showers everything with loose earth. The same weight of explosive packaged in a different way can be made to do more damage in the form of a cluster bomb, which scatters a large number of small submunitions (bomblets) over a wide area. There are British, American, French and German, not to mention Soviet versions of the weapon.

The RAF's BL755 cluster bomb weighs 600lb

80 Mirage F.1 with Matra Magic air-to-air missile on its wingtip and a laser-guided glide bomb on the underwing pylon. (*Photograph courtesy Matra*)

(272kg) and contains 147 bomblets. When the main bomb is dropped armed, the static line attached to the pylon snatches and begins the fusing sequence. A small propeller vane at the nose of the weapon spins up until it registers an airspeed of 275 knots (317mph), then a gas balloon inflates, causing the bomb shells to separate and scattering the bomblets. A stabilizing vane pops out at the back of each bomblet, plus another spinning vane which rotates five times to arm the system which is, in turn, fired by a spring-loaded piezo-electric crystal at the nose upon impact.

These bomblets will wreak havoc among personnel, buildings or soft-skinned vehicles. The rear part of the casing fragments, but most of the energy of the shaped-charge warhead is used to produce a jet of very hot gas which can burn a hole in thick armour-plate. A copper lining behind the charge melts and completes the damage.

It is the 'thermic lance' effect of the shaped-charge warhead which makes it so effective, but if tank armour is constructed of a sandwich with a heat-proof ceramic middle layer, as is the frontal armour of the Russian T-72, then the bomblets will have very little effect.

The American Rockeye 20 scatters 8in. (20cm) steel darts and the CBU58 cluster-bomb unit is filled with over 600 circular bomblets each smaller than a tennis ball, ridged so that they spin in flight and so arm themselves. The French use the Giboulee dispenser or, alternatively, the Matra Beluga cluster bombs, but the most amazing submunitions dispenser of all is the Luftwaffe's MW-1 Streuwaffen which takes up almost the whole of a Tornado's flat belly. This pack can eject 112 separate bomblets sideways, and there is a choice available between armour-piercing weapons, anti-tank seismic mines, or anti-airfield weapons.

FAE Weapons

Napalm firebombs have been used since World War II and have acquired a horrific reputation, but napalm's modern successor, the FAE (Fuel-Air Explosive) is even more effective, particu-

81 Alpha Jet with Beluga cluster bombs. (*Photograph courtesy Matra*)

82 Jaguar carrying four cluster bombs. (*Photograph courtesy British Aerospace*)

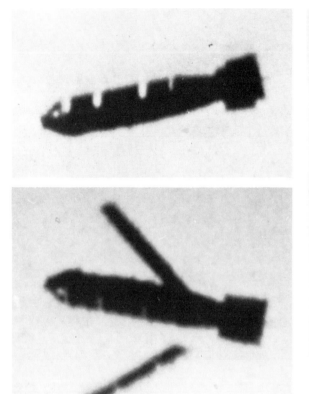

83 Cluster bomb sequence. (*Photograph courtesy British Aerospace*)

larly against tanks. A half-tonne FAE bomb produces an aerosol cloud of methane or a similar inflammable gas, mixed with air, and then ignites it. The resulting fireball and shockwave can disable tanks over a wide area.

Anti-Airfield Weapons

Many an East Anglian farmer will tell you how difficult it is to make much impression on the concrete of a World War II runway. In trying to knock out an airfield in wartime, special bombs must be used against the runways; ordinary HE bombs cause little damage, and even that can be repaired quickly by suitably trained and equipped Rapid Runway Repair (RRR) teams.

The Matra Durandal anti-runway bomb is a 'concrete dibber'. It is released at low level in the ordinary way but is slowed by its drogue parachute until it hangs almost vertically. Then a rocket fires to hammer the steel-nosed bomb into the runway at more than 800ft (250m) per second. After one second the main charge explodes under the concrete, producing a crater 16ft (5m) wide and 6ft (2m) deep, sur-

84 F-15E Strike Eagle demonstrator carrying Durandal anti-runway bombs, Sidewinder missiles and a conformal FAST (Fuel and Sensors Tactical) pack along the fuselage sides. (*Photograph courtesy Matra*)

85 GAU-8/A Avenger seven barrel Gatling gun capable of firing 70 rounds per second of 30mm ammunition. In the background is the aircraft which carries this fearsome close-support weapon, the Fairchild Republic A-10 Thunderbolt.

rounded by a large shattered area. Repairing this kind of damage could take days.

The RAF will soon have available the JP233 anti-airfield weapon which will be carried as a Tornado belly-pack in the same way as the MW-1. This fires charges into the runway like the Durandal, but also scatters the airfield with hundreds of small mines and delayed action anti-personnel weapons, hindering repair work even further.

AIR-TO-AIR MISSILES

Most people are fairly familiar with the basic idea of heat-seeking, air-to-air missiles, such as the Sidewinder, which home in to the infra-red heat radiation produced by the jet exhaust of their targets. Other types of missiles home in on radar energy reflected by their targets, or are guided by radioed commands from the parent aircraft, or use their own active radar to find their targets, or any combination of these methods. The general impression seems to be that all the attacking pilot has to do is to get his target more or less in his sights and press the button. Whereupon the missile is fired with a 'whoosh' and sets off in hot pursuit of its target which is almost certain to be destroyed because there is no way that a manned aircraft could hope to out-manoeuvre a missile. To a certain extent, this is true enough. The heat-seeking missile is a deadly weapon when used correctly.

86 Tornado carrying MW-1 Streuwaffen weapons dispenser. (*Photograph courtesy Panavia Aircraft GmbH*)

The Sidewinder

The Sidewinder AIM-9L can accelerate up to Mach 2.5, turn at up to 30 'g', and chase its quarry for over 11 miles (18km). When it catches it, the warhead explodes with enough energy to destroy quite a large aircraft. It is used at short ranges and is what could be described as a 'fire and forget' missile. It is firing the missile in the first place which presents the pilot with problems. Unless the seeker head of a Sidewinder has locked onto the heat from the target's exhaust before it is fired it will streak away from the parent aircraft and try to shoot down the sun.

Sidewinders are carried on a launcher-rail unit which fits on to the standard underwing pylon connections. The missile is fitted into the rail by means of two small shoes, clips grip the canard steering vanes at the front of the Sidewinder, and an umbilical multi-pin connector cable is plugged in. When the missile has been selected and armed, this cable becomes extremely busy relaying information between the missile, the pilot and the radar. The umbilical cable also carries a thin hollow line through which liquid nitrogen passes from a reservoir bottle at the rear of the launcher attachment.

87 Sky Flash and Sidewinder air-to-air missiles carried on underwing pylons by Saab J37 Viggen of the Swedish Air Force

This liquid nitrogen is used to cool the metal surrounding the missile's heat-seeking head to a temperature of 77°K. Once armed, the seeker-head begins to scan, looking for a heat source on to which to lock. It searches along the aircraft boresight and then scans in a cone around this area. The pilot can slave the seeker head to a target identified on radar or use a movable marker on his HUD to show the seeker where to look. Once satisfied, the seeker will lock on and a tone will sound in the pilot's headset. Now he can press the button on his joystick to fire the missile. The seeker will maintain lock all the way to the target, transmitting steering commands to the missile's canard foreplanes.

When the button is pressed, the rocket motor ignites, pushing the missile forward out of its launcher rail and guillotining the electric umbilical. The missile is now on its own and has to rely for power on a small generator driven by gas from the rocket motor. It is not a 'ballistic' missile, but a small pilotless aeroplane, relying for lift on fixed cruciform wings at the rear interacting with canards at the front. Stability is provided by ingenious slipstream-driven, 'rolleron', gyroscopic devices at the tips of the rear wings.

The first heat-seeking, air-to-air missiles were fired in anger as long ago as 1958. These early missiles, including the earliest Sidewinders, were little better than cannon. Their acquisition-cone was very narrow; they could only lock on to and be fired at targets already lined up with the launch aircraft's boresight. If the target aircraft could manage to 'break' violently enough into a tight turn, the pursuing missile could lose its lock on the target and go off chasing the sun.

The first Soviet heat-seeking missile, the K-13 (NATO codename AA-2 Atoll) was copied from the early Sidewinders whose faults it reproduced. US fighter pilots gained valuable experience Atoll-dodging in Vietnam but, since then, both US and Soviet heat-seeking missiles have been upgraded to such an extent that the approach to air combat is totally different, and the lessons learned in Vietnam are no longer completely relevant today.

The Sidewinder has been improved in a number of ways. The best-known current version is the Sidewinder AIM-9L. This has an expanded-acquisition mode which allows it to seek and lock onto heat sources even at large 'off-boresight' angles. It features improved cooling, a more sensitive seeker which locks on more quickly and is better at maintaining lock, and an on-board computer which can estimate 'lead' and turn the missile very quickly so as to aim *ahead* of a crossing target. Such missiles are a completely different proposition to the earlier 'pursuit-course' Sidewinders and Atolls which had to be fired from the classic 'tail-chase' position astern of their targets. The new missiles can be fired 'beam-on' at targets crossing ahead, or even 'head-on' at approaching targets. The pilot just 'points' the parent aircraft at the target, in order to obtain a lock-on, then fires. An agile fighter such as the F-16 with its

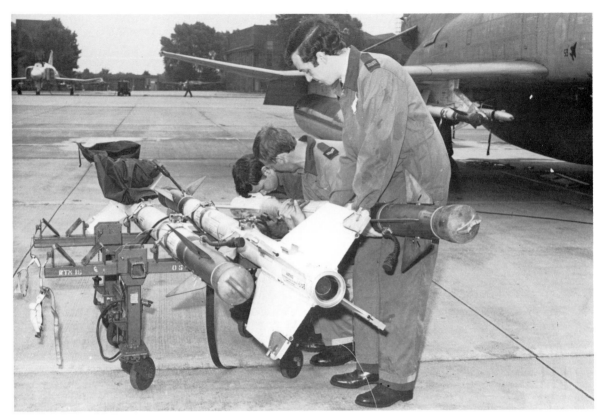

88 Armourers with AIM-9 Sidewinders at RAF Wattisham. In the background is a Phantom FGR.2. The plastic caps covering the missile-seeker windows are removed before flight. Note also the stabilizing 'rollertrons' at the missile wingtips. (*Photograph courtesy RAF*)

ability to change direction quickly to point its nose almost anywhere in the sky may make the best launch platform for these new, 'all aspect', heat-seeking missiles. They can be fired from almost any angle and cannot be outmanoeuvred. Nor will they go off chasing the sun. The only possible countermeasure would be to fly *very* low or to use decoy flares, but even these might well be useless against a later version of the Sidewinder which will be able to distinguish between the heat from the target and that from a flare.

Advanced Short-Range Air-to-Air Missile (ASRAAM)

An Anglo-German partnership is developing a new heat-seeking missile – ASRAAM (Advanced Short-Range Air-to-Air Missile) which should replace Sidewinder in the 1990s. The new ASRAAM will have even further expanded acquisition and improved manoeuvrability, plus the ability to lock on to a target even *after* it has been launched. Target acquisition by means of helmet-pointing, already deployed on anti-tank helicopters, will take ASRAAM-equipped fighters almost into the realms of 'thought control' as depicted by Craig Thomas in his best-selling novel *Firefox* (Michael Joseph, 1977). Sensors above the pilot's head will estimate which way his helmet is 'looking' and relay commands to the missile seeker, even by radio datalink should the ASRAAM be already on its way. We may be certain that some or all of these improvements will be copied by future versions of US, French, Israeli and Soviet air-to-air missiles.

Already, most of the current air-to-air missiles have an all-aspect or very-nearly-all-aspect capability as compared with their predecessors; the Soviet K-13A Advanced Atoll, AA-3 Anab, AA-6 Acrid, AA-7 Apex and

AA-8 Aphid, plus the French Matra Magic 2 and the Israeli Shafrir 2 and Python 3. The older versions of these missiles are now obsolete.

It is becoming more and more likely that the outcome of an air-to-air combat will be decided on the first pass, without waiting for a reeling, tail-chasing dogfight to develop. In future air battles, opposing fleets of fighters will fire their missiles at each other head-on at maximum range. Other things being equal, they will shoot each other down on a one-to-one basis, giving victory to the side which put up the larger number of fighters. This kind of air combat would certainly favour the Warsaw Pact's 'can-non-fodder' tactical philosophy, based as it is on possessing large numbers of simply equipped fighters, rather than the NATO philosophy of concentrating on technological excellence.

Long- and Medium-Range Radar-Guided Missiles

However, the philosophy of technological ex-cellence is not dead yet. One way of escaping the deadly outcome described would be to develop missiles which could engage their targets at ranges far greater than would ever be possible using heat-seeking missiles. These are essentially short-range missiles and cannot achieve a reliable lock-on at ranges greater than a few miles. Long- or medium-range air-to-air missiles have to rely on some other form of guidance, namely radar.

Already, the primary armament of most air-defence fighters is not cannon, nor even Side-winders, although both of these are fitted. The primary armament of the F-4 Phantom, the F-14 Tomcat, the F-15 Eagle and the F-18 Hornet is the AIM-7 Sparrow radar-guided missile, which has a range of at least 25 miles (40km), while the RAF's Phantoms and Tornado F.2s, plus Swe-den's JA37 Viggen are armed with the British Aerospace Dynamics Sky Flash – an improved version of the Sparrow. Both of these missiles are described as Medium-Range (MR) Semi-Active Radar Homing (SARH), and the fighters armed with them expect to use them to engage targets which are still too far away to be seen or identified by eye, hence the other buzzword description of these missiles – BVR (Beyond Visual Range). Fighters would be expected to deal with as many targets as possible by using

their medium-range missiles (Fox One), then as the range shortened they would use their sec-ondary armament (Fox Two) of short-range, heat-seeking missiles such as Sidewinder or ASRAAM. Finally, as the range shortened still further and fighters could swing in behind their targets, they could probably find an oppor-tunity to use their cannon (Fox Three).

The problem with using missiles such as the Sky Flash, Sparrow and even longer range (125 miles [200km] and more) AIM-54 Phoenix to best advantage, i.e. at long range, particularly at night and in bad weather, is the problem of identification. Is the blip on the radarscope an attacking 'hostile' or a returning 'friendly'? Pilots have to rely on a system known as IFF (*see p.59*) to provide an electronic password to aid recognition. Almost all aircraft, both military and civil, carry IFF transponders to enable them to transmit the coded passwords, and the sys-tem is of great benefit in air traffic control.

This is only one end of the IFF system and, until recently, only ground-based radar and fighter controllers possessed the other end which has the means of decoding which pass-word replies indicated friendly aircraft. Now the larger fighters (F-15, Tornado F.2) and the AEW planes (Boeing E-3A, Nimrod AEW.3) carry IFF interrogators integral with their radars for decoding IFF passwords which 'label' a target as either friendly or hostile, but the system still worries NATO commanders. Heavy enemy jamming and spoofing could degrade IFF almost to the point of unusability in any real war, so reliance on long- or medium-range radar-guided missiles presents other problems.

The guidance system used by these missiles, SARH, is supposed to work as follows. With the Sparrow and Sky Flash, the launch aircraft is required to lock its radar on to the target to keep it 'illuminated' all the time the missile is in flight, while the missile itself homes in on the reflected radar energy. This is by no means a 'fire and forget' system. Not only must the parent aircraft continue to fly towards the target in order to keep it illuminated, becoming increasingly ex-posed to enemy missiles as the range de-creases, but, as its radar is locked on to one single target all this time, it is unable to scan and is therefore 'blind' to other targets. Should the enemy try to use jamming, the radar must

89 Four BAe Dynamics Sky Flash medium-range missiles under the belly of the prototype Tornado F.2. (*Photograph courtesy British Aerospace*)

switch frequencies and signal the changed frequency over a radio datalink to the missile.

There are a number of techniques in being or in the pipeline which would avoid the dangerous need for the parent aircraft to keep flying towards the target for illumination purposes. Rearward-facing radars are one suggestion which has yet to be tried. The US Navy's F-14 Tomcat fighter can launch up to six long-range Raytheon AIM-54 Phoenix missiles almost simultaneously, each at a separate target up to 100 miles (160km) away. Each Phoenix flies on autopilot until it can locate and home in on its assigned target using its self-contained active homing radar.

Advanced Medium-Range Air-to-Air Missiles (AMRAAM)

The disadvantage of the Phoenix missile is its size 13ft (4m) weight (nearly half a tonne) and expense. Its advantage is that it can be fired and forgotten. Perhaps the ideal compromise will be the new Sparrow replacement, the Hughes AIM-120 AMRAAM (Advanced Medium Range Air-to-Air Missile) Like Phoenix, AMRAAMs are designed to be launched against several targets simultaneously from a fighter equipped with TWS (Track While Scan) radar. This uses a radio datalink to keep each missile updated on its target's position until the AMRAAM is close enough to use its active radar homing. Should the target try to jam this, AMRAAM can switch in a 'home-on-jam' mode, or switch repeatedly between active radar and home-on-jam. AMRAAM will overcome many of the present limitations of Sparrow and Sky Flash missiles and will eventually arm most NATO fighters, including the Tornado F.2, the F.16 and the Sea Harrier. Both of the latter will require new TWS radars if they are to reap the benefit.

Unlike the Sidewinder, Sparrow, Sky Flash, Phoenix and AMRAAM are not fired along a rail, but launched from an ejector similar to an ERU. An explosive charge operates a long-stroke piston with a force up to 4 tonnes, breaking the retaining shear-pins and pushing the missile well down and clear of the launch aircraft.

AIR-TO-SURFACE MISSILES

Again, these use a variety of guidance systems.

90 Mirage 2000 fires a Matra Super 530 medium-range, radar-guided, air-to-air missile. (*Photograph courtesy AMD-BA*)

Wire-Guided

Anti-tank missiles fired from helicopters, such as the Hughes TOW (Tube-Launched, Optically Tracked, Wire Guided) and the Euromissile Hot (Haut-Subsonique, Optiquement Téléguidée, Tiré d'un Tube), are wire-guided by means of a system described as CLOS (Command to Line-of Sight). The gunner aboard the helicopter keeps the crosshairs of his stabilized telescopic sight lined up on the target while an infra-red source on the rear of the missile is used to 'gather' it into the line-of-sight by transmitting steering commands along the wire, which is unreeled from a drum on the launcher. These missiles have a range of about 2½ miles (4km).

Laser-Guided

Laser-guided missiles such as the Rockwell Hellfire, which arms the AH-64 Apache advanced attack helicopter and can also be fitted to other helicopters such as the Westland Lynx, do not have the drag-producing limitation of a trailing wire. The Apache's TADS (*see p.62*) aims a narrow beam of invisible laser light at the target, which scatters it in all directions enabling the Hellfire to home in on the reflected laser energy.

The laser seeker developed for the Hellfire missile is also used on other weapons, such as LGBs and the Laser Maverick missile. The Hughes AGM-65 Maverick is, in reality, a family of missiles, each with differing guidance heads and all of them designed to be launched from fixed-wing aircraft. The AGM-65A and AGM-65B are TV-guided, the AGM-65D and -F are IIR-guided (Imaging Infra-Red) versions and the AGM-65E is the Laser Maverick.

TV-Guided

TV Mavericks are equipped with seeker heads which provide the pilot with a narrow-field-of-view image of the target area on his cockpit CRT screen. He aligns the crosshairs on the selected target or aiming point and gives the missile a few seconds in which to 'memorize' the details of the scene, noting shapes, patterns of contrast, etc. on to which it will thereafter remain locked. Maverick is indeed a very intelligent missile, and once it has locked-on and fired, can be forgotten about as it speeds to the visual target printed on its memory.

Imaging Infra-Red-Guided (IIR)

IIR Mavericks work on the same principle, except that what the pilot sees on his screen is now a thermal image of the target, enabling the missiles to be used at night. Working on the known fact that Warsaw Pact tank crews are training to move and fight at night, the US Air Force has recently placed a very large order for more than 60,000 IIR Mavericks, the now-favoured version of a missile which has already scored a better than 85 per cent kill probability in tests and live action.

Unpowered Glide Bombs

Unpowered glide bombs are a possible alternative to powered missiles. They can be designed to use the same seeker and guidance systems as the missiles, trading off the missile's range against the ability of the glide bomb to carry a much heavier warhead, approaching a tonne in the case of most glide bombs. The Paveway LGB and Matra BGL glide bombs are laser-guided. The GBU-15 and HOBOS (Homing Bomb System) weapons are TV- or IIR-guided but, instead of using a memory as in the case of the Maverick, the 'image' of the target is datalinked back to the launch aircraft.

Anti-Shipping Missiles

Anti-shipping missiles are launched along a compass heading, then switch to active radar guidance when they get close to their targets. Recently, the Exocet has become something of a byword for anti-ship missiles but, besides being easy to decoy, the 40 mile (65km) range of this sea-skimmer hardly compares with the 68 mile (110km) range of the McDonnell-Douglas Harpoon or the British Aerospace Dynamics Sea Eagle, both of which are used by the RAF and the Royal Navy. The longest range anti-ship missiles are those carried by surface ships, such as the SS-N-12 which arms the *Kiev* and *Slava* class warships. These have a range of at least 312 miles (500km) and rely for their accuracy on precise, mid-course targeting updates

being provided by an aircraft or helicopter remaining discreetly concealed just beyond the radar horizon. The Soviet Navy uses versions of the Kamov shipboard helicopter or the Tupolev Tu-142 land-based aircraft to provide this OTHT (Over the Horizon Targeting) facility. Without it, the missiles could be too easily decoyed away from the real target into a cloud of 'chaff'.

RAF anti-shipping Buccaneers are equipped with both the Sea Eagle and the smaller (and older) Martel anti-shipping missiles. One version of Martel is TV-guided (via a datalink), while an alternative version can home in on the target ship's radar.

Anti-Radar Missiles

The best-known anti-radar missile is the Shrike, which is designed to 'suppress' anti-aircraft defences by homing in on radars and destroying them. It is effective also against powerful radios and jammers, but Shrike has always had an annoying flaw in that, if the radar being attacked saw it coming, it could switch off and the missile would then miss.

Israel was able to use Shrikes to knock out Syrian air-defence radars in the Bekaa Valley in 1982, and a squadron of Shrike-equipped Phantom F-4Gs of the US Air Force is based at Spangdahlem in West Germany. These are the 'Wild Weasels', dedicated to defence suppression. The F-4Gs carry a number of radar-warning devices which would enable them to pinpoint hostile emitters. They would approach these very low and as closely as possible, before releasing their Shrikes, giving the radar operators the minimum time to switch off their equipment or to employ counter-measures.

However, newer and better anti-radar missiles are on the way. The Spangdahlem Wild Weasels will soon replace their Shrikes with HARM (High-Speed Anti-Radiation Missile). HARM is more intelligent, and can seek out emitters which have just switched off or which happen to be locked on to a target instead of scanning. Both HARM and its British counterpart ALARM (Air-Launched Anti-Radiation Missile) which will be carried by Tornadoes, have a mode in which they can climb to 40,000ft (12,000m) then 'loiter' by dangling beneath a parachute while they search for emitters. Finally, they dive on to their chosen targets.

91 **Sea Harrier armed with Sea Eagle missile.** (*Photograph courtesy British Aerospace*)

SURFACE-TO-AIR MISSILES

Aircraft are under threat from Surface-to-Air Missiles (SAM). These exist in great variety, ranging from hand-portable weapons such as the Stinger, Shorts Blowpipe, Soviet SA-7 Grail and the new French SATCP (Sol-Air Très Court Portée) Mistral – capable of providing ground troops with reliable protection against attacking aircraft over very short ranges – through Rapier, Roland, Chaparral and Crotale – used to provide SHORAD (Short-Range Air Defence) for airfields and other tactical installations – to the larger Hawks and Bloodhounds which have a long-range, high-altitude capability. Stinger has infra-red homing and is said to be particularly effective against helicopters; Blowpipe is radio controlled by the operator using a thumbball, while Rapier is CLOS (*see p.101*) with Blindfire radar tracking for use in low cloud or at night. The bigger missiles use SARH (*see p.99*). Shipboard missiles such as Seawolf use CLOS with TV or radar tracking. The British Aerospace Seawolf is effective against aircraft, sea-skimming missiles and has even intercepted a $4\frac{1}{2}$in. shell. There is a famous story of a signal from the Royal Navy frigate which fired the shell to the frigate which launched the Seawolf: 'I see we have just shot down your missile!'

6 The Strategy of Deterrence

It is the rivalry between the two Superpowers with their respective allies which provides most of the impetus for the development of the military aviation technology outlined in previous chapters. While both blocs claim that they are committed to the ideals of Peace and Friendship, they are unsure how far they can trust one another, so the arms race continues unabated.

The Soviet Union was invaded by Hitler's Germany in 1941 and in the ensuing 'Great Patriotic War' 20 million Soviet citizens died. But the Russians fought back, chasing the retreating Germans all the way to Berlin and beyond and, in the process, 'liberating' countries such as Poland, Czechoslovakia, Hungary and the Balkans from Nazi oppression while setting up regimes sympathetic to themselves. In the late 1940s a Soviet 'empire' stretched from the Arctic to the Adriatic, and there was grave danger that other European states still weak and recovering from the horrors of war might be added to that empire. It was in response to this fear that the North Atlantic Treaty Organisation was born in 1949. The treaty provided for mutual defence on the principle that 'an attack on one is to be regarded as an attack on all'. The members of NATO at the present time are the USA, UK, West Germany, Norway, Belgium, Holland, Denmark, Spain, Portugal, Italy, Luxembourg, Greece, Turkey, Canada and Iceland. France left the unified NATO command structure in 1966 in order to pursue an independent foreign policy, but still remains sympathetic to the Alliance. Meanwhile, the Soviet Union felt threatened by the NATO grouping and arranged a series of bilateral defence treaties with its European client states – Poland, East Germany, Hungary, Romania, Czechosolvakia and Bulgaria – which came to be known collectively as the Warsaw Pact.

The Soviet Union has formidable armed forces, including air forces and a navy with a worldwide role, which many people see as being far in excess of what is needed for the defence of the Soviet Union or her allies. The Soviets, on the other hand, see the defence of their homeland and of their brand of Socialism as their most important national purpose. Never again are they going to be caught almost defenceless as they were by Hitler in 1941 and, if they have to fight, their strategy will be to attack. They have in place in Eastern Europe very large numbers of troops, tanks, armoured fighting vehicles, and tactical aircraft, all of which would be used to push the front edge of the battle westward should the need arise.

Many people think that if there is another war in Europe it will take the form of a nuclear holocaust which will turn the Northern hemisphere in general, and Europe in particular, into a radioactive desert. However, if war ever does break out it is more than likely that there will be at least an intitial period when so-called 'conventional' weapons will be used, and in its ability to wage a conventional war at the present time the Warsaw Pact is arguably much better equipped than NATO. The key to European security does not lie in nuclear weaponry but in equipping NATO forces with the ability to defeat the Russians in any conventional phase of a war; to stop their tanks in their tracks. To deter against any possible military adventures on the part of the Warsaw Pact it is necessary for NATO to make it clear that such adventures would bring no benefits to the Soviets, only enormous risks. A credible deterrent must be not only nuclear but also conventional, and in 1967 NATO abandoned the previous stance of Massive Retaliation, or MAD (Mutually Assured Destruction), and switched instead to the doctrine of Flexible Response. Any use of force against members of the Alliance would be responded to by the appropate level of counterforce. For this doctrine to be a credible deterrent, it must be made clear that NATO has the men, the equipment, the training and the resolve to defend itself wherever and in whatever way it is attacked. In practice, deterrence means that NATO must be able to prevent a war by being ready at all times to fight one.

Comparisons between NATO and Warsaw Pact forces are not just a simple matter of counting planes, tanks or warheads. They are complicated by the fact that NATO's strongest member, the USA, has most of its forces on the 'wrong' side of the Atlantic and would need to ship these to Europe in time of war across an ocean full of hostile submarines. The Warsaw Pact, on the other hand, needs only to drive a few hundred miles in its tanks.

The Warsaw Pact relies heavily on mobility and firepower, and a battle in Western Europe would involve very large numbers of tanks, supported by helicopters and tactical aircraft. Its strategy would be to push westwards as quickly as possible in order to overrun West Germany, Holland, Luxembourg, Belgium, Denmark, Scandinavia and possibly France, before people realized what was happening and the politicians could arrange a truce. On their southern flank they would hope to overrun Greece, Turkey and possibly Yugoslavia. To the north, they would try to capture the north Cape of Norway and, if neutrals such as Sweden or Finland got in the way, they would be elbowed aside.

NATO's counter-offensive would depend heavily on using the UK as an offshore aircraft-carrier for the reinforcement of Europe and as a base for tactical air strikes. Although the air defence of the UK presents problems, it could probably be assured easily enough during the early days of the war. Meanwhile, another battle would be taking place in the Atlantic and the Western Approaches between NATO navies and those of the Soviet Union.

SOVIET AIR POWER

The organization of the Soviet Air Forces is explained by the broader aspects of Soviet strategy as outlined above. The largest of the air forces is Frontal Aviation or Tactical Aviation with 5000 tactical aircraft and some 3500 helicopters. Other air forces are Long-Range Aviation, Naval Aviation, Military Transport Aviation and an entirely separate air force assigned to Air Defence and equipped with SAM missiles, chains of radars and the latest interceptors. Other tactical air forces are operated by most of Russia's East European satellites.

Soviet aircraft types are named from the 'Experimental Design Bureaux (OKB) in which they originate. These design bureaux are known usually by the name of their leading designer, past or present, e.g. Mikoyan, Sukhoi, Tupolev, etc. Each new design is given a number, e.g. MiG-21 and as improvements or modifications are made to the basic type, suffix letters are used: e.g. MiG-21SMT. For many years NATO has adopted the practice of assigning each new type an unflattering reporting codename: e.g. F indicating fighter, e.g. 'Flogger'; B for bomber, e.g. 'Blinder' and so on.

The popular image of Soviet aircraft production is of factories working like unstoppable machines once a new design has been flight-tested and approved, turning out MiG-21s at the rate of dozens per week and unable to modify the basic 25-year-old design. But this is not quite what happens. The MiG-21 appears to be a good airframe with a lot of life left in it and, because the Soviet Union is not a 'throwaway' society, the early models go back to the factory to be refurbished, and emerge later with improved engines, avionics, weapons systems, performance and capabilities. The truth is that most of Frontal Aviation's 5000 tactical aircraft are less than ten years old and they are being modernized all the time.

Another popular myth is that Russian aircraft are unsophisticated. It is a known fact that, although research and development in the Soviet Union is fairly well organized, they lag behind in certain fields, such as micro-electronics, when compared with the West. But, whatever the reasons for this 'technology gap', the Russians are determined to close it, and one of the quickest ways of catching up is to copy Western ideas, such as air-to-air missiles and tactics. Imitation is more than just a sincere form of flattery, it is also the quickest way of getting a working model through the prototype stages

Soviet Military Aircraft

Soviet Designation	NATO Reporting Codename	Roles
ANTONOV		
An-12	Cub	Transport (Cub-A), Elint (Cub-B) ECM (Cub-C) and ASW
An-22 Antheus	Cock	Long-range transport
An-400	Condor	Long-range giant transport
BERIEV		
Be-12 Tchaika	Mail	MR and ASW flying boat
ILYUSHIN		
Il-18	Coot	ECM and Elint
Il-38	May	MR and ASW
Il-76	Candid	Long-range transport, utility and heavylift transport, ECM
Il-76	Mainstay	AWACS
KAMOV		
Ka-25	Hormone-A	Shipboard ASW helicopter
Ka-25	Hormone-B	OTHT helicopter
Ka-25	Hormone-C	Utility shipboard helicopter and SAR
Ka-27	Helix-A	Shipboard ASW helicopter
Ka-27	Helix-B	OTHT helicopter
MIKOYAN-GUREVICH		
MiG-21F	Fishbed-C and E	Day interceptor
MiG-21PF	Fishbed-D	All-weather interceptor
MiG-21FL	Fishbed-D	Export MiG-21PF
MiG21PFM	Fishbed-F	All-weather interceptor
MiG-21R and RF	Fishbed-H	Tactical reconnaissance
MiG-21PFMA and MF	Fishbed-J	Multi-role fighter/ground attack
MiG-21SMT	Fishbed-K	Multi-role fighter/ground attack
MiG-21bis	Fishbed-L	Multi-role fighter/ground attack
MiG-21Mbis	Fishbed-N	Multi-role fighter/ground attack
MiG-21U	Mongol	Two-seat trainer
MiG-23M and MF	Flogger-B	All-weather interceptor
MiG-23U	Flogger-C	Two-seat trainer
MiG-27	Flogger-D	Single-seat ground attack
MiG-23	Flogger-E	Export MiG-23MF
MiG-23BN	Flogger-F	Export MiG-23/27
MiG-23MF	Flogger-G	Modified MiG-23MF
MiG-23BN	Flogger-H	Modified export MiG-23/27
MiG-27	Flogger-J	Single-seat ground attack
MiG-25	Foxbat-A	Interceptor
MiG-25R	Foxbat-B	Reconnaissance
MiG-25U	Foxbat-C	Two-seat trainer
MiG-25R	Foxbat-D	Reconnaissance
MiG-25M	Foxbat-E	Low-altitude interceptor
MiG-29	Fulcrum	Look-down/shoot-down interceptor
MiG-31	Foxhound	Look-down/shoot-down interceptor

Soviet Military Aircraft *Continued*

Soviet Designation	NATO Reporting Codename	Roles
MIL		
Mi-2	Hoplite	Light utility helicopter
Mi-4	Hound	Utility (Hound-A), shore-based ASW (Hound-B), and ECM (Hound-C) helicopters
Mi-6	Hook	Heavylift transport helicopter
Mi-8	Hip	General purpose transport and assault helicopter (Hip-C), ECM (Hip-D), anti-armour (Hip-E) and export anti-armour (Hip-F)
Mi-14	Haze	Amphibious and ASW helicopter
Mi-24	Hind-A,D,E,F	Assault, attack and anti-armour helicopters
Mi-26	Halo	Heavylift transport helicopter
Mi-28	Havoc	Advanced attack helicopter
MYASISHCHEV		
M-4	Bison	Long-range bomber and flight-refuelling tanker (Bison-A), MR (Bison-B, C)
SUKHOI		
Su-7	Fitter-A	Single-seat ground attack
Su-11	Fishpot-C	Interceptor
Su-15	Flagon	All-weather interceptor
Su-17	Fitter-C, D	Single-seat ground attack
Su-17	Fitter-E, G	Two-seat trainer
Su-17	Fitter-H	Multi-role and ground attack
Su-20	Fitter-C	Export Su-17 (Fitter-C)
Su-22	Fitter-F	Export Su-17 (Fitter-D)
Su-22	Fitter-J	Export Su-17 (Fitter-H)
Su-24	Fencer	Interdiction strike
Su-25	Frogfoot	Battlefield close-support
Su-27	Flanker	Look-down/shoot-down interceptor
TUPOLEV		
Tu-16	Badger	Medium-range bomber (Badger-A) missile launcher (Badger-B) anti-shipping missile launcher (Badger-C, G) Elint (Badger-D, J) Reconnaissance (Badger-E, K) ECM (Badger-H)
Tu-22	Blinder	Medium-range reconnaissance (Blinder-A), Missile launcher (Blinder-B), maritime (Blinder-C) and trainer (Blinder-D)
Tu-22M	Backfire-B	Supersonic strike and reconnaissance
Tu-?	Blackjack	Long-range supersonic strike
Tu-95	Bear	Long-range bomber (Bear-A) and missile-launcher (Bear-B)
Tu-126	Moss	AWACS
Tu-28 and 128	Fiddler	Long-range interceptor
Tu-142	Bear	Maritime strike (Bear-C), Elint and OTHT (Bear-D), MR (Bear-E), ASW (Bear-F)
YAKOKLEV		
Yak-36	Forger	Shipboard VTOL fighter

93   MiG-25R tactical reconnaissance aircraft. (*Photograph courtesy Fotokhronika Tass*)

94   Pilots of the Carpathian Military District with their MiG-23MF all-weather multi-role fighters. (*Photograph courtesy Fotokhronika Tass*)

and into production. It is worth remembering also that in some fields the Russians have several years lead over the West – for example, the use of space for military purposes, high-power lasers and similar 'death-ray' weapons, tank design, and the mass-production of large turboshaft engines for helicopters.

The safest thing to assume is that Soviet aircraft are just as capable as their NATO counterparts, that their pilots are just as well trained and that their command structures are just as effective. Comparisons are not easy to make because we in the West are not given the opportunity to learn much about the Soviet air forces or their equipment. Soviet fighters are exported world-wide, but not always in the latest and best-equipped versions. The later versions of the MiG-21 showed up well in combat against F-4 Phantoms in Vietnam, but the Libyans and Syrians do not seem able to get the best out of their Fitters and Floggers in combat with either the F-14 Tomcats of the US Navy, or Israel's F-16s.

Besides being widely exported, Soviet aircraft types are built under licence in a number of countries. Poland builds the Mi-2 helicopter under licence and has designed the PZL-Mielec Iskra trainer and a number of small transports. MiG-21s are produced in China and India. China builds the Tu-16 bomber under licence, and India is now preparing to produce the MiG-23/27 side-by-side with licence-built Jaguars. Czechoslovakia has designed and built the Aero L-39 Albatross trainer, and there are a few 'home-grown' trainers and light attack aircraft flying with the air forces of Yugoslavia and Romania powered by Rolls Royce Viper engines.

No assessment of Soviet air power would be complete without a mention being made of the huge civil airline Aeroflot. In the event of war, this airline could be requisitioned rapidly to airlift troops and supplies. The Tu-134 airliner is well known, and is particularly suited to landing large numbers of combat troops on forward airfields. Many Tu-134s still have a glazed nose, which would be occupied in wartime by a tactical observer/navigator, and all have large, low-pressure tyres which are ideal for landing on makeshift or recently repaired runways. Furthermore, the undercarriage legs retract backwards into a nacelle on the wings and are capable of taking bumpy runways and pot-holes in their stride, thanks to the shock-absorber which is built into the trailing struts on each leg.

NATO AIR POWER

In NATO language, Warsaw Pact forces are not spoken of as 'the Enemy' but as 'the Threat'. Following a period of supposed detente which ended with the Soviet invasion of Afghanistan in December 1979, NATO politicians woke up to the disturbing realization that while they had wasted ten years in cutting defence budgets and failing to modernize, Threat forces had been steadily strengthened and upgraded during this period. By contrast, the 'eighties have been marked so far by a resolve on the part of all NATO members to increase defence spending in real terms and to deploy new and more effective weapons systems, such as Tornado. There has also been a move towards standardization, with more commonality and interchangeability at every level, whether it be personnel or equipment.

NATO's command structure for the defence of Western Europe is ACE (Allied Command Europe) based at SHAPE (Supreme Headquarters Allied Powers Europe) near Mons in Belgium. ACE is divided into three regional commands; Northern, Central and Southern. Northern covers Scandinavia, where the air forces of Norway and Denmark are included in the overall command structure. They are busy at present modernizing their equipment, notably by taking delivery of the General Dynamics F-16 Fighting Falcon to replace older types such as the F-104G Starfighter, the Saab J-35 Draken and the Northrop F-5E. There are no US or Canadian bases, although units of the Royal Canadian Air Force would deploy to Norway in an emergency.

The Central Region is defended by the Second and Fourth Allied Tactical Air Forces. 2ATAF comprises the air forces of Belgium and the Netherlands, RAF Germany and parts of the Luftwaffe. 4ATAF consists of the rest of the Luftwaffe, and units of the USAF and Canadian Air Force based in Germany. The aircraft entrusted with the defence of this crucial region are the most modern and best-equipped in NATO: the F-16s operated by the Netherlands

95   A Boeing E-3A of the NATO AEW Force touches down at its base at Geilenkirchen, Germany. Notice the NATO insignia and the Luxembourg crest and serial on the fin. (*Photograph courtesy NATO AEW Force*)

and Belgium (and built under licence by Fokker at Schiphol and by a Belgian consortium at Gosselies), the McDonnell-Douglas F-15 Eagle, plus the Panavia Tornado in the all-weather interdictor strike role. RAF Strike Command does not form part of 2 or 4 ATAF but is entrusted with the defence of the airspace around the UK, stretching from Iceland to the Baltic. In time of war, Britain would serve as a vast unsinkable aircraft carrier and important strike units of the RAF and the USAF are based here. France, although not officially part of the NATO command, would presumably be fighting on the same side in any large European war, and is equipped with a large air force which includes the new Mirage 2000.

NATO's Southern Region comprises Portugal, Italy, Greece, Turkey and now Spain, which has recently joined the Alliance. Phantoms have formed the backbone of the Spanish, Greek and Turkish Air Forces, with Spain operating a number of other types including Mirage F-1s and shipboard AV-8A Harriers. Greece and Portugal operate the Vought A-7 Corsair II in the strike role, and Italy expects to receive 100 Tornadoes. The remarkable, multi-role, single-seat fighter/strike F/A-18 Hornet has been chosen by Canada and Spain and Australia as part of their re-equipment programmes. In Spain's case it was a choice between the Hornet and the Tornado, with the Hornet being chosen finally.

All this equipment is matched by a C³I infrastructure which includes a chain of radar stations stretching from Norway to Turkey known as NADGE (NATO Air Defence Ground Environment) and complemented by other radar chains in Britain (UKADGE) and elsewhere. The possibility of a surprise attack is made less likely by the deployment of AEW aircraft, such as RAF's Nimrod AEW.3 based at Waddington but capable of operating from other bases, and the Boeing E-3A AWACS. The E-3As, whose main operating base is Geilenkirchen, are

96 The onboard systems of the E-3A are operated by multinational crews. (*Photograph courtesy NATO AEW Force*)

unique in NATO in that they are the only aircraft owned and operated by the Alliance as a whole. They fly in NATO insignia with Luxembourg serials and are manned by multinational crews. Both the Boeings and the Nimrods carry advanced look-down pulse Doppler radar capable of detecting low-flying aircraft against ground clutter, IFF interrogators for distinguishing between friend and foe, and ESM systems (Electronic Surveillance Measures) which detect, locate and classify different radio and radar emissions.

NATO is justly proud of the way in which the various national air forces and military personnel throughout the Alliance have learned to work together. This is something that could not have been easily foreseen 30 years ago, and there is little doubt that they could fight together if they have to. A large part of NATO's efforts are given over to joint manoeuvres and tactical exercises, and the aircraft of different air forces

frequently deploy to each others' air bases as part of routine training.

The most important exercise designed to test the preparedness of a NATO base is the TACEVAL (Tactical Evaluation). This takes place with a minimum of fore-warning and for several days the entire base goes on to a war footing, even down to the wearing of NBC clothing.

If there is going to be a conventional war, it will probably be preceded by a period of tension lasting several weeks, during which NATO units could be redeployed or dispersed. Saboteurs would attempt to infiltrate NATO air bases and to destroy radio and radar installations throughout the countryside. If the politicians could find no means of cooling the tension, there would be tremendous pressure on both sides to launch a surprise attack. NATO is primarily defensive and would probably prefer to wait until the Threat forces struck. It is likely that the outbreak of hostilities would be at night or in bad weather.

97   A brand new F-16 for the Royal Netherlands Air force about to be delivered from the assembly plant at Schiphol. (*Photograph courtesy Fokker*)

98   Spanish Air Force Mirage F-1. (*Photograph courtesy AMD-BA*)

99 Operating from roads and dispersed bases is a technique regularly practised by the Swedish Air Force. (*Photograph courtesy Saab-Scania*)

100 The US Marines and the air forces of Spain, Canada and Australia are re-equipping with the F/A-18 Hornet multi-role fighter. (*Photograph courtesy McDonnell-Douglas*)

AIR SUPREMACY

A clear Warsaw Pact objective would be to establish air supremacy over the Central European battlefield from Day One. Surprise attacks would be launched against NATO airfields by a variety of Soviet counterair types, such as the MiG-23BN Flogger and Su-17 Fitter. These would hope to destroy NATO aircraft on the ground, crater runways, smash hardened shelters and spray the entire airfield with toxic chemicals. However they would need to get through first.

The first warning of a surprise air attack would come from the look-down radars of the Boeing E-3As, able to detect low-flying aircraft out to 250 miles (400km). This would give anything up to 20 minutes warning of attacks on NATO airfields – sufficient time to scramble the Phantoms of the Luftwaffe and RAF Germany, the F-16s of the Dutch, Belgian and Danish Air Forces, the USAF's F-15 Eagles, plus a useful assortment of F-5s, Drakens, Starfighters, etc. In the ensuing dogfights these would expect to be outnumbered by vast formations of attackers. Outnumbered, perhaps, but not outgunned. The Allied fighters hope to achieve a better than one-to-one kill ratio because they carry more missiles and because the newer fighters, such as the F-15 and F-16, are supremely agile. Other differences, such as better radars and better-trained pilots might also count in the Allies' favour, but a big plus is the excellent dog-fighting reputation enjoyed by the F-16 and its more powerful brother the F-15. Both are ideal Central Region fighters.

The Eagles, Falcons, Tigers and Phantoms could not expect to knock all the Floggers and Fitters out of the sky. Enough would get through to pose problems for the SAM and SHORAD radar and missile systems, for any aircraft left behind on the ground at allied airfields, and for the airfields, bridges, troop concentrations, communication lines and any other targets of military value. The attackers would try to get through by a combination of very low flying and heavy ECM jamming. Was it not Marshal Ogarkov who is reputed to have said: 'We aim to shoot down 30 per cent, jam out another 30 per cent and then our victory is assured'? Certainly, heavy jamming plays an important part in the overall Soviet tactical philosophy, as does the policy of having large numbers of individual aircraft. Radio communication, radar, both airborne and ground-based, and in particular IFF, would be jammed and spoofed to the point where their usefulness would be seriously compromised, while the Soviets remain philosophical about their own systems being

101 Dual-role F-15E Strike Eagle of the US Air Force. This aircraft would use its LANTIRN podded sensor system to seek out armour and other ground targets well behind enemy lines while still being able to defend itself using Sidewinder air-to-air missiles.

jammed in a similar way. They are much less worried than the West about their IFF, for example, being degraded to the point where they will even shoot down their own returning aircraft. They can afford to lose a few planes and pilots in this way. The West cannot.

While NATO's fighters were being scrambled to deal with the intruders, a counterstrike consisting of F-111s, Tornadoes, Jaguars, Phantoms, etc. would be on its way to disable Warsaw Pact airfields and installations. The F-4G 'Wild Weasels' from Spangdahlem would knock out radars using HARM missiles, while F-111s attacked airfields under the protection of EF-111 'Raven' tactical jammers. Tornadoes would be armed with the JP-233 anti-airfield weapons, while they protected themselves with Sky Shadow ECM jamming pods and ALARM anti-radar missiles. They would be flying at extremely low level and would take a variety of detours to avoid known SAM and radar sites. All these aircraft would then hope to return to their bases in the West and to find strips of concrete long enough to land on, refuel and re-arm before setting out again.

The vulnerability of NATO airfields in Europe is a cause for concern, and many people advocate the dispersal of aircraft to strips of road, to secondary grass airfields, or the use of VSTOL fighters such as the Harrier. Dispersal is not as easy as it sounds, and the presence of heavy trucks, refuelling tankers, etc., plus the muddy tracks they leave, would tell the enemy where to look. The traditional notion of the 'Harrier Hide' as a carefully camouflaged clearing in a forest is giving way to newer forms of concealment using urban areas, disused factories, etc. After all, where better to hide a machine than among other machines?

Britain's airfields, both civil and military, would be prime targets for the Warsaw Pact Su-24 Fencers and Tu-22M Backfires, and the task of defending these airfields would fall to the RAF. An advantage which the UK possesses is that attackers would be detected quickly as they tried to cross the North Sea. Nimrod AEW.3s would provide the early warning and Tornado F.2s on CAP would be the first line of defence, followed by the RAF's Phantoms. Both of these types would depend on air-to-air refuelling from airborne tankers. Close-in air defence would be provided by Lightnings, still very fast and capable interceptors, even if they lack endurance, and, in daylight, by Hawks armed with Sidewinders and flown by instructors. SAM missiles such as Bloodhounds and SHORAD missiles such as Rapier would provide an additional defensive cordon.

102 The Sukhoi Su-24 *Fencer* is capable of attacking targets in the UK from its bases in Eastern Europe

103 Sidewinder-armed Hawks would provide the RAF with a useful additional daylight air-defence capability. (*Photograph courtesy British Aerospace*)

THE AIR-LAND BATTLE

As far as Warsaw Pact strategy was concerned, all the foregoing would be a mere preliminary to the main show, which would be to capture as much Western territory as possible, as quickly as possible. At any time the politicians might call a truce and the Soviets would like to be left in possession of a large slice of Western Europe as some small recompense for their troubles.

The flat plains of Northern Germany are ideal tank country, and the 'Big Red Machine' would waste no time in taking advantage of this. The tanks would immediately start to roll westward. Any points of resistance would be by-passed, or encircled and mopped-up later. The tanks would carve a way through for other forms of mechanized armour: self-propelled guns and missile batteries, personnel carriers and mobile command posts. Operational Manoeuvring Groups endowed with a great deal of tactical independence would use helicopters to leapfrog forwards in order to sabotage bridges, supply depots, etc. This would make it very difficult for NATO to turn the tide of the invaders' advance. What mainly operates in NATO's favour is the sheer number of Warsaw Pact weapons which would be needed for a successful *Blitzkrieg*. Many tanks and fighting vehicles would certainly get bottled-up at a river-crossing or other 'choke-point', unable to move; a perfect target for a large-scale 'turkey shoot' using what ever weapons come to hand; cluster bombs, FAE weapons, the A-10 and its mighty cannon, artillery, and so on.

Anti-Tank Helicopters

A more open battlefield would bring the assault helicopter into its own. The Russians have the Mi-8 Hip and the Mi-24 Hind each packing a lot of aerial firepower. Western assault helicopters tend to be smaller, but carry more sophisticated weapons systems. The US Army's AH-1 Cobras based in Germany carry eight wire-guided TOW anti-tank missiles with shaped-charge warheads, plus a triple-barrelled gun and rocket projectiles. This ordnance is delivered using such sophisticated devices as helmet-pointing for rapid target-acquisition, a gyro-stabilized telescopic sight and laser-ranging. The British Army's Lynx is more of a utility heli-

copter, but in its later versions and adaptations it is becoming a dedicated tank-killer, armed with HOT or TOW missiles.

The Hughes AH-64A Apache is the most sophisticated anti-tank helicopter yet to enter service. In the knowledge that the Russians will probably use the cover of night or bad weather to move forward their tanks, Hips and Hinds, the US Army's new Apache has all-weather capability, with infra-red sensors for locating targets at night, a laser-designator for marking those targets and up to 16 Hellfire laser-homing missiles for destroying them. The Apache will also carry Sidewinders for use against hostile helicopters.

Although helicopters are very vulnerable to anti-aircraft missiles, small arms fire, and even to wire-guided anti-tank weapons, they may offer the best hope of stopping a sudden armoured thrust by the enemy. They are faster than any tank and can get ahead of the column by flying 'nap of the earth' to keep out of sight, taking advantage of shallow valleys, belts of woodland and even rows of buildings. They can lie in ambush and wait for the tanks to show themselves, knowing that they have much better all-round vision than the crew of the tank. Hit-and-run tactics would be used because, after firing a missile, it would be most unwise for a helicopter to sit around and invite attention from the tank's main gun. Better for the Lynx, Cobra or Apache to keep on the move, hoping to score another shot later.

Helicopters have many other uses during a land battle. The Gazelle or the OH-58 Kiowa can be used for scouting or observation, passing target information to the gunships. Utility helicopters such as the UH-1 Huey, UH-60 Blackhawk, Westland Puma, Lynx or Commando can ferry troops and their equipment or evacuate casualties. Heavylift helicopters, such as the Boeing Vertol Chinook or Mi-26 Halo, can airlift guns, radars, ammunition or missile batteries to wherever they are needed.

Because the Russians will be using helicopters such as the Hip and the Hind, heavily armed and capable of wreaking havoc among Allied personnel and equipment – even helicopters – a new twist of complexity is being given to the air-land battle strategy: the anti-helicopter-helicopter, fighter helicopter, or LHX-SCAT (Light Helicopter Experimental-Scout and Attack) as the project is already known. LHX will be the basis of a whole new family of US light helicopters, but the SCAT version should be the most interesting, capable of achieving air supremacy at very low level over the entire battlefield area, with the speed, agility and quick reactions necessary to neutralize any threat and dodge any missile fired at it. The new design will employ a great deal of leading-edge technology and, until it is ready, NATO must consider a number of short-term possibilities for dealing with the Hinds – scout helicopters armed with Sidewinders or Stingers, light aircraft, small fighters such as the Hawk and Alpha Jet, and man-portable anti-aircraft missiles; these have all been advocated.

Close-Support Strike Aircraft

Fixed-wing aircraft such as the Jaguar, F-16, Harrier and A-10 would be available to provide close-support during a battle. The essence of successful close-support operations is to keep away from the FEBA (Forward Edge of Battle Area) until sent for. An air strike would be called in either by the ground commander himself directly or relayed by a Forward Air Controller from an observation aircraft such as the Rockwell OV-10 Bronco. For maximum effectiveness, close-support strike aircraft have to loiter until required, preferably in the vicinity of an in-flight refuelling tanker, or, in the case of the Harrier, wait in a well-concealed 'hide'. Both the Harrier and Jaguar have as their chief weapon the BL755 cluster bomb, while the A-10 mounts a GAU-8/A Avenger 30mm seven-barrelled cannon and a total of 11 weapons pylons. The A-10 can sustain a considerable amount of battle damage and still fly; the pilot sits in a titanium-armoured bathtub. However, the A-10 was not originally designed for all-weather operations and most A-10s are likely to be fitted with the LANTIRN pod (*see p.62*) in the near future.

Although the Warsaw Pact nations have enough tanks to station one of them every 10yd along the present frontier, they would not be able to use all of them at once, and NATO's best hope of fighting them to a standstill might be to attack the 'second echelon' or 'follow-on' reinforcements as they move up to the front. These reinforcements would be most likely to move at

104   US Army AH-1S Cobra helicopter gunship stationed in Germany, showing launch tubes for TOW wire-guided, anti-tank missiles and container for 2¾in. rocket projectiles

105   Front cockpit of AH-1S Cobra gunship showing eyepiece of telescopic sight, selector controls for TOW missiles, laser ranger and VHF tactical radio

106   TOW-armed Lynx demonstrates how to stage an ambush. (*Photograph courtesy Westland*)

night or under heavy cloud cover, and the best hope of spotting them would be to use some kind of wide aperture, high-resolution radar, such as the Pave Mover system, which could be carried by an aircraft such as the F-111. This would detect armoured columns on the move, and targeting information could be passed to a missile or an aircraft which would dispense what are known as 'terminally guided sub-munitions'. Essentially these are small 'smart' missiles, each with enough 'brainpower' to recognize a tank either from the infra-red heat signature or from a picture built up using millimetre-wave radar. They would have the added advantage that they would hit the tank on the top where its armour is thinnest rather than on the heavily armoured front or sides.

The concept of fighting this kind of Air-Land Battle 2000 sometime in the future in defence of Western Europe is so complex that many lay people are left thoroughly confused and (if they happen to be on the front line, as are the Germans) probably quite scared. To integrate all one's efforts, air power, anti-tank weapons, scout helicopters, assault helicopters, utility and radio-relay helicopters, fighter helicopters, ground forces, armour, supplies, logistics and C^{3}I – is a difficult enough task in a peacetime exercise. If war were to break out, no easy victory could be assured; there are too many uncertainties. This kind of war has never been fought before. Although there are opportunities to test some of the equipment and tactics in small-scale wars from time to time, it is to be hoped that the risk and uncertainty involved in a full-scale World War will remain great enough to deter either side from taking the initiative.

KEEPING THE SEALANES OPEN

Unlike Warsaw Pact second echelon forces, NATO reinforcements would have to cross the Atlantic, thereby running the gauntlet of Admiral Sergei Gorshkov's Soviet Navy. The threat to Allied shipping is a multiple one, coming from submarines, surface warships and the long-range aircraft of Soviet Naval Aviation. Soviet warships are capable of firing very long-range sea-skimming missiles, such as the SS-N-12 which has a reputed range of more than 300 miles (600km) and would find its target with a little help from a small shipboard helicopter or a long-range 'fleet-shadower' such as the Tupolev Tu-142 *Bear-D*. Bears can themselves launch long-range anti-shipping missiles, and submarines would attack either with torpedoes or missiles. Some submarines can launch their missiles from underwater; others have to surface first.

Anti-Submarine Warfare

The 'war' against submarines goes on even in peacetime. NATO anti-submarine operations in the North Atlantic are directed from Pitreavie Castle in Scotland where the objective is to track every single Soviet submarine which ventures from its base in the Kola Peninsula round Norway's Nordkapp into the Atlantic or towards the Mediterranean. Arrays of listening devices called SOSUS (Sound Surveillance System), strung out along strategically important sections of the ocean bed, register the passage of submarines. Once the submarine has triggered a SOSUS chain and has passed out into the open ocean, the job of tracking it is taken over by maritime patrol aircraft such as the Lockheed P.3 Orion, the Dassault-Breguet Atlantique or the RAF's Nimrod MR.2.

Nimrods

The Nimrods are based at Kinloss in Scotland and St Mawgan in Cornwall. Each of these large aircraft, descended from the Comet airliner, carries a crew of 12 in airline comfort. They are trained to work as a team, but each is a specialist in operating some part of the Nimrod's complex equipment which is used not only for anti-submarine operations but also for routine maritime patrols and mercy missions such as Search and Rescue.

Typically, a Nimrod will leave Kinloss and use the power of its four Spey turbofans to get it quickly and at high altitude to one of its routine task areas, such as the Greenland-Iceland-Faroes-UK gap. It may be taking over from a previous patrol aircraft which has been tracking a suspected submarine contact and, on reaching the task area, it will shut down two of its Speys and loiter on the remaining two for up to nine hours on task, circling above the sea at medium or low altitude at a speed of 250-300

knots (288-345mph). During Operation Corporate, the 1982 Falklands War, a number of Nimrod MR.2s were fitted with a flight-refuelling probe which enabled them to fly 19-hour sorties from Ascension Island, patrolling off the coast of Argentina. For self-protection the Nimrods also carried AIM-9L Sidewinders and Harpoon antiship missiles. But in North Atlantic operations protective air cover would be available and the missiles should be unnecessary.

Diesel-electric submarines have to surface to charge their batteries, but it is rarely that a 'snorting' Soviet submarine will allow itself to be caught by a Nimrod. The Nimrod's high-resolution Searchwater radar will sketch clearly the profiles of surface shipping and will also detect a submarine periscope. However, alongside the periscope there will always be an ESM antenna listening out for radar emissions and, as soon as it picks up those of the Nimrod, the submarine will dive. Minutes later the Nimrod will arrive overhead to begin dropping a pattern of sonobuoys spaced about 2½ miles (4km) apart. Alternatively, the Nimrod could be tasked with attending to the sonobuoys dropped by a previous aircraft.

A sonobuoy is a passive listening device consisting of an underwater microphone, a VHF transmitter and antenna. It floats almost completely submerged so that it cannot be detected easily on radar, and when its batteries are exhausted (after about 8 hours) it is designed to

sink without trace. Davy Jones presumably has an extensive collection of only slightly used sonobuoys.

Anything a sonobuoy hears is transmitted back to the Nimrod. Noise made by fish is a nuisance, but there may be some mechanical noise there also: the motors of diesel-electric submarines or the very noisy cooling pumps of the nuclear-powered variety. Each sonobuoy uses a separate channel in the band – 136-173.5 MHz – and the Nimrod circles above its pattern of buoys, homing-in with the aid of a VHF direction-finder on each in turn in order to update its position on the navigator's tactical display screen. Meanwhile, highly trained sonics operators use their ears plus a device called Jezebel to analyze the noises coming from the buoys, concentrating on known frequencies and resonances. The submarine may not know that it is being listened to as it tries to make good its escape, and when it passes close to a sonobuoy the noises it makes, as recorded by the pen-traces of the Jezebel, will show a Doppler shift at the closest point of approach. Stalking submarines from a Nimrod requires great skill, teamwork and patience, and it may take the crew several hours to pinpoint a submarine or to re-locate one which has 'escaped' by changing its speed or direction.

There is another passive method of detecting a submarine which involves recording disturbances in the earth's magnetic field known as

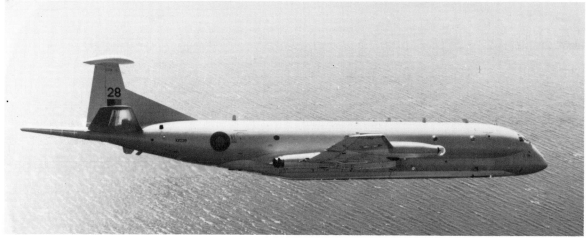

108 and 109   Maritime patrol aircraft designed mainly for anti-submarine operations. Both types have now been refitted with new sensors and processing equipment. Dassault Breguet Atlantique 2. (*Photograph courtey AMD-BA*)
109   Nimrod   MR.2.   (*Photograph   courtesy   British Aerospace*)

110   Royal Navy Sea King HAS.5 anti-submarine helicopter demonstrates its 'dunking' sonar. (*Photograph courtesy Westland*)

magnetic anomalies. A submarine, being a large chunk of ferrous metal, may, under certain conditions, cause a detectable disturbance in the magnetic vectors being monitored by the Magnetic Anomaly Detector (MAD) device which is housed in the Nimrod's long tailcone. This provides further evidence of the presence of a submarine.

Active sonar is used to send a 'ping' through the water which will be reflected by any submarine nearby, giving an instant read-out of its range and direction, but it will also alert the submarine, possibly for the first time, to the fact that it is being hunted. In wartime a Nimrod would use an acoustically homing torpedo to attack a submarine.

The Nimrod carries a crew of two pilots, a flight engineer, two navigators, one Air Electronics Officer, three sonics operators, a radio-teletype operator, a radar operator and one MAD/ESM operator. Seating is available for spare personnel as required. There is a galley and toilet and a large area for the carriage of sonobuoys, flares, liferafts, etc. The two navigators share the roles of routine navigation of the

111 Compact sonics processing suite aboard the Royal Navy's Sea King HAS.5, consisting of Marconi LAPADS and AQS-902 signal processor. (*Photograph courtesy Marconi Avionics Limited*)

aircraft and operation of the tactical plotter displayed on a large CRT screen. This screen interfaces with the radar, the navigation system and the autopilot and provides a computerized tactical display which can be used to show surface vessels, sonobuoys, etc., and to steer the aircraft under autopilot to the next point of interest.

Ship-Board Helicopters

The Royal Navy uses helicopters carried on board ships in the anti-submarine role. The Lynx equips the smaller ships and also undertakes the general duties of a shipboard helicopter, whereas the Sea King HAS.5 is a dedicated and specialized sub-hunter. Its equipment compares with that of the Nimrod, although there is clearly less room and the crew is smaller. The Sea King's radar is the MEL Sea Searcher which

can interface with a Doppler-fed TANS (Tactical Area Navigation System) to provide a combined radar, navigation and tactical display. Sonobuoys are dropped as with the Nimrod and monitored via the Marconi LAPADS (Lightweight Acoustic Processing and Display System) which is similar to Jezebel. Unlike a Nimrod, a Sea King can hover while 'dunking' an active sonar. A MAD device is carried in the starboard sponson and trailed below the Sea King when it is in use. Other equipment carried by the HAS.5 includes an Orange Crop ESM set and Mark 44 or 46 homing torpedoes.

When the fleet is at sea in wartime escorting a convoy, or during an exercise, frigates will patrol in a fan ahead of the main carrier group, searching for submarines. Sea Kings from the carriers will patrol ahead of the frigates and lay down flank barriers of passive sonobuoys parallel with the line of the fleet's advance. Under present-day conditions of ASW (see p.52) it would be necessary to keep a swath of sea up to 200 miles (320km) each side of the fleet clear of enemy submarines. Meanwhile, the threat from the air would require an equally far-seeing lookout, provided in Atlantic waters by the radars of Orions, Nimrods and Atlantiques. Deprived of airborne radar cover during the Falklands War, the Royal Navy hastily adapted a number of Sea Kings to carry Nimrod-type Searchwater radars. This is in contrast to the carrier-escorted task groups of the US Navy which always embark Grumman E-2C Hawkeye AEW planes.

Aircraft Carriers

During any war in the North Atlantic it would be necessary to deal with any long-range airborne threat coming from Soviet air bases in the Kola Peninsula to the north-east of Finland, including Tu-16s, Tu-22Ms and Tu-142s. These would be intercepted by Royal Navy Sea Harriers or by the US Navy's Tomcats, and destroyed using medium- or long-range missiles.

There is now a clear difference between the way the Royal Navy operates, with its light carriers taking Sea Harriers and helicopters, and the large carriers of the US Navy which are able to carry a whole range of fixed-wing aircraft, each tailored to a specific purpose. The latter's air defence is provided by the large and

112 A Super Etendard about to be catapulted from the French carrier *Clemenceau*. (*Photograph courtesy AMD-BA*)

113 A Grumman A-6E Intruder comes home to the USS *Nimitz*, arrester hook about to engage. (*Photograph courtesy US Navy*)

114 Aircraft lashed-down on the storm-swept decks of HMS *Hermes* during the Falklands War which earned the Harrier its spurs and proved the validity of the light carrier concept. (*Photograph courtesy Royal Navy*)

potent F-14 Tomcat which has Mach 2.5 performance and is capable of launching 125 mile (200km) range Phoenix missiles. These should be able to deal with any approaching airborne threat to the Fleet, and the threat itself would be detected by E-2C Hawkeye AEW radar planes, constantly on patrol. Strike capability is provided by a mixture of A-6 Intruder and A-7 Corsair attack aircraft and protection against enemy radars is provided by the EA-6 Prowler airborne jammer. There is a fixed-wing ASW aircraft in the shape of the Lockheed S-3 Viking. This carries homing torpedoes, depth charges, mines and sonobuoys and, also relies on MAD and Flir sensors to find its target. The job of delivering important spares, personnel and equipment to a carrier at sea is accomplished by the Grumman C-2A Greyhound, used exclusively for COD (Carrier on-board Delivery) though, at one time, the US Navy was studying the purchase of Fokker F-28 Fellowship jet-liners for this job.

Flying high-performance, fixed-wing aircraft on and off carriers is an exacting task, even though the steam catapult is invariably used to get airborne and arrester gear to get back on deck again. Land-based, fast jet pilots would baulk at the thought of landing their planes on a carrier, for unlike landing on a runway, it is not possible to round out the approach into a gentle 'flare' hoping to touchdown at the right moment; the deck simply isn't long enough. The Tomcat pilot aims to hit the deck at the approach speed and angle, even though he may be dropping at 16ft (5m) per second – a punishing descent for any undercarriage. But there is no need to worry about bouncing – once the hook engages the arrester wires, the Tomcat is immediately pulled to a grinding halt.

Compared to this, the job of the Sea Harrier pilots is easy. A gently accelerating roll up the ski-jump into forward flight gets them airborne and they land in a straight vertical descent, facing into the wind over the deck. The Sea Harrier/light carrier combination proved itself in the Falklands War, the great advantage of these carriers being that they were able to embark a number of the RAF's GR.3s flown by pilots who had never landed on a carrier

115 The Soviet warship *Kiev* with Yak-36 *Forger* VTOL fighters amidships and an assortment of missile launchers on the foredeck

before. Even the Sea Harrier complement was reinforced by aircraft transported to the South Atlantic aboard a container ship, the planes taking off vertically from the container deck and transferring to the carriers.

The Soviet Navy also uses the light carrier concept. The *Kiev* now has two sister ships, the *Minsk* and the *Novorossiisk*, each of which embarks a squadron of Yak-36 Forger VTOL fighters. These Forgers invite comparison with Sea Harriers but, instead of a single vectored-thrust turbofan, as in the Harrier, the Forger has three engines. Two of them point vertically downward and are used only for vertical landing and take-off. In flight they are pure dead weight and probably account for the limited warload which the Forger can carry. Nonetheless, the Forger gives the Soviet Navy a useful interceptor/strike capability which it previously lacked.

116 RAF Harrier GR.3 on an exercise over northern Norway. (*Photograph courtesy RAF*)

Anti-Shipping

Operations against Soviet surface warships which threaten Allied shipping would be undertaken either by carrier- or land-based strike aircraft. Soviet warships are, however, well protected by surface-to-air missiles guided by tracking radars. The most widely used Allied anti-ship missile is the McDonnell-Douglas Harpoon, which has a range of about 69 miles (110km) and is powered by a rocket motor. The British Aerospace Sea Eagle has an air-breathing jet engine, enabling it to have even greater range, but exactly what this range will be is still classified. Sea Eagle also has, besides active radar homing, a microprocessor brain which will enable it to distinguish the real target from decoys and jamming. Sea Eagle will be carried by Royal Navy Sea Harriers and RAF Buccaneers.

The anti-ship missile carried by the Tornadoes of Germany's Marineflieger is the Kormoran, the effectiveness of which would be vital in preventing the Baltic from becoming just another Russian lake from which seaborne assaults on Denmark and the North German coast would be made. The Soviets would also be quick to invade and sieze the Nordkapp region of Norway, an area which they see as vital to their continued mastery of the Barents Sea and the security of their bases around Murmansk and throughout the Kola Peninsula. Units of the Soviet Navy's Northern and Baltic Fleets would try to rendezvous off Norway and prevent NATO forces getting through. Today, both Soviet and NATO navies use the Norwegian Sea for large-scale peacetime manoeuvres, and each winter combined NATO forces including a detachment of RAF Harrier GR.3s providing close support train in the harsh environment of the Norwegian mountains. Apart from their obvious training value, these exercises are a big boost to Norway's morale and a signal to any would-be aggressor that there are no quick and easy victories to be won. This in many ways is the essence of deterrence: an insurance policy against ever having to cross swords in anger.

117 Lockheed S-3A Viking shipboard ASW aircraft. (*Photograph courtesy US Navy*)

7 *Tactics and Training*

Deterrence depends upon people as much as it does upon machines. The training given to pilots, for example, must be of the highest order, ensuring that in the heat of battle the trained pilot will automatically apply the skills and tactics he has learned. However, there is a danger that training could become too rigid and mechanical, leaving the pilot with little or no initiative or tactical independence. Such a pilot would be scarcely better than an automaton, and the two million pounds required to train each pilot might be better spent on buying missiles.

RECRUITMENT AND INITIAL TRAINING

The Royal Air Force has a very long and thorough training programme, and the excellence of RAF fast jet pilots is often attributed to this. The RAF trains not only its own pilots, but Royal Navy fixed-wing pilots also, and space is found on training programmes for small numbers of overseas pilots. Young men and women between the ages of 17 and 23 should apply to their local RAF careers Office. If they meet the required entry standards they are passed to the Officers and Aircrew Selection Centre at Biggin Hill where they undergo a rigorous battery of individual and group tests designed to test flying aptitude, personal and social qualities. These tests are designed to screen out misfits and candidates who would be difficult to train. Before investing the best part of £2 million on training, the RAF has got to feel reasonably convinced that it is going to get its money's worth and that the pilot is not the type to crash and get killed, so writing off an expensive aircraft on his first major expedition. However much a young person may want to fly a fast jet, he is wasting his time if he has not got the mental and physical qualities needed to stand the strain.

Six months are spent learning to be an officer in the RAF before the student pilot gets anywhere near a real aeroplane. He will then move to one of the Basic Flying Training Schools at Linton-on-Ouse, Leeming, or Church Fenton, all of which are situated in the flat and fertile Vale of York, drained by the Rivers Swale and Ouse and threaded by the A1 Great North Road.

It is on the Jet Provost, that the RAF pilot learns his basic airmanship: take-offs, circuits, landings, low-speed handling, going solo, plus a certain amount of night and instrument flying. It takes a whole year which includes all the usual ground school work: aerodynamics, weather, navigation, etc. At the end of the year the students are streamed – some to learn to fly or navigate multi-engined aircraft at Finningley, others to helicopters at Shawbury, while the much-envied 'fast jet' stream go to fly Hawks at the Advanced Flying Training School at Valley on Anglesey. Six months are spent here, notching up 72 hours on the red-and-white Hawks, and sharpening up on their skills; flying low and fast, cross-country, navigational exercises and the beginnings of air-to-air and air-to-ground tactics. At the end of the Valley course the Wings ceremony is held, when the students receive the coveted wings badges which mark them out as fully trained pilots, and when they cease to be the direct concern of the RAF's Flying Training Command.

THE TACTICAL WEAPONS UNIT

The Tactical Weapons Units at Brawdy in Dyfed and Chivenor in Devon are administered by RAF Strike Command. As at Valley, Hawks are flown, but these are camouflage-painted and

118 A Hawk from the RAF's Advanced Flying Training School, Valley, Anglesey. (*Photograph courtesy British Aerospace*)

are equipped to carry weapons. Although the British Aerospace Hawk is an excellent trainer, it is much more besides. It is no mere toy aeroplane, and in the weapons-training role it really comes into its own, outperforming every comparable aircraft doing the same job, even the Franco-German Alpha Jet. One very important advantage possessed by the Hawk is that the instructor can supervize weapons delivery by looking over the student pilot's head, where he has much the same view through the ISIS sight as the student himself. It was this quality, combined with the planes ruggedness and economy that led to a version of the Hawk with strengthened undercarriage for deck landings, being chosen to train US Navy pilots. The Hawk makes a formidable daylight ground-attack aircraft, and can even be used in the air-defence role where its fuel-thrifty Adour turbofan enables it to loiter on CAP for as long as two and a half hours.

In the front seats of the Brawdy and Chivenor Hawks, RAF pilots are trained to fight. They fly to weapons ranges such as the one on the Pembrey marshes near Llanelly to deliver their bombs, rockets and gun attacks. The Pembrey

target is easy enough to see – a large sheet of white painted plywood in the centre of a ring of white drums – but it is far from easy to hit. The Hawk pilot is using only a straightforward ISIS reflector bombing sight without any help from radar altimeters, laser rangefinders or digital computers. Later in his flying career he may graduate to ground-attack aircraft such as Jaguars, Harriers or Tornadoes, which are equipped with all of these sophisticated aids to accurate bombing, but for the time being he learns his trade the hard way – from the bottom up. As he makes pass after pass to deliver yet another practice bomb or burst of gunfire at the sheet of plywood, the ISIS camera records how well he has taken aim and the spotter on the range is able to note where his weapons impact, and record the success, or otherwise, of his efforts.

Not all sorties from the Tactical Weapons Units carry live weapons. Much time is spent flying across country, weather permitting, navigating at low level to carry out a SAP (Simulated Attack Profile) against some perfectly innocent target. Again, this is done the hard way – no sophisticated navigation systems or projected map displays. The trainee plans his route by tracing it out with marker pens on a map. Minutes into the flight are marked and compass

119 Hawk trainers from the Tactical Weapons Unit, RAF Chivenor in north Devon on which student pilots learn to use weapons. (*Photograph courtesy British Aerospace*)

headings for each leg of the run. Then he takes the map or a section of it with him. This is flying by map, compass and stopwatch at an altitude of around 250ft (76m) and a speed of 400 knots (461mph). The RAF receives regular complaints about the nuisance caused by low-flying jets. In order to diversify to some extent the nuisance value, the whole of the UK is used as a low-flying playground, the exceptions being controlled airspace, and the vicinities of certain towns, hospitals etc. A square marked by the pilot on his map indicates the initial point (IP) from which he starts his 'bomb run' proper towards the marked triangle denoting the 'target'. This can be any suitable landmark – a bridge, country railway station or electricity pylon. Again, the ISIS camera provides the only evidence that it has ever been 'attacked'. No weapons were used, only film. Other unarmed

sorties from the TWUs are used to teach pilots the basics of air combat.

AIR COMBAT

Rare qualities must be possessed by a pilot if he is to survive and score victories in the deadly kill-or-be-killed 'game' of aerial combat. The rules or tactics of this game vary, depending on the type of war being fought, the mission being flown, the types of aircraft taking part, the effectiveness of their radars and missile systems, etc. Contrary to what many people may suppose, there is no definitve 'Bible' of tactics or dogfighting manoeuvres to be learnt first, and the fledgling fighter pilot will have to wait until he joins his first squadron before he can get to grips with the finer points of combat tactics. The initial part of his air combat training takes place at Brawdy or Chivenor, teaching him the basic skills and principles involved, and enabling both him and his instructors to judge whether he has the necessary aptitude and qualities for successful air combat.

The first of these important requirements is good eyesight and the ability to use it. Four out of every five aircraft shot down in combat never even see their attacker. Rule One therefore is: keep your eyes open and, in particular, watch your Six o'Clock, i.e. the zone behind your tail. From here an attacker can most easily sneak up unseen, lock on a missile or bracket you with close-range cannon-fire. Hawks from the Tactical Weapons Units chase each other in mock dogfights, hoping to outmanoeuvre their 'opponents' and record a 'kill' with their gunsight cameras. In these wheeling, looping engagements, tomorrow's fighter pilots slowly perfect other skills and requirements, such as situational awareness – the ability to know where you are and where everybody else is and what they are doing in a confused mêlée, where everybody strives to keep and hold the initiative, and where to relax one's concentration, to become predictable or to fail to keep a lookout astern is to lose. All this, plus constant physical discomfort from pulling high 'g' in tight turns, near blackouts, strained neck muscles from continually looking around, makes up the essential training of a fighter pilot. Not every novice takes to it or makes the grade.

There is also the routine training, such as the

120 Close-up of F-16 showing the all-round view enjoyed by the pilot. (*Photograph courtesy Marconi Avioncs Limited*)

tail-chase, where one Hawk chases another round the turns trying to keep it in its gunsight; the cine-weave, which is a tail chase with the gunsight camera running, or the firing of live cannon rounds at a towed target, usually a large canvas banner. The techniques of aerial fighting have changed over the years, particularly recently with the advent of all-aspect missiles, but the basic principles and requirements remain the same. Keeping a sharp lookout is as important as ever, so is situational awareness, and so too is good flying ability.

In the days of cannon and the early missiles limited to pursuit courses, attacks had to be staged from the rear. The attacker's best ally was the element of surprise – 'bouncing' an opponent before the latter knew what was happening. If the opponent did see the attack coming, his best defence was to 'break', i.e. to manoeuvre sharply, either vertically or to one side. The attacker then had to follow round the turn and, in order to bring his guns or missiles to bear, he had to be able to turn more tightly than his opponent. Thus we get what is often thought of as the 'classic' dogfighting situation: two aircraft chasing each other round a tight turn. The victory would go to whichever aircraft had the advantage in speed or turning ability. In a tight turn the wings are working very hard, often quite close to the stall. High-lift devices such as slats are useful, and as the drag builds up considerably, the engines must be powerful enough to prevent too much loss of speed.

Aircraft performances differ: some are powerful, others less so: some turn better because of

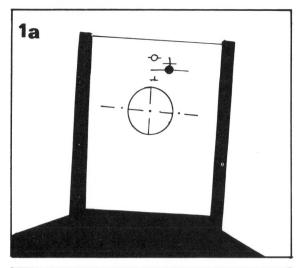

1a

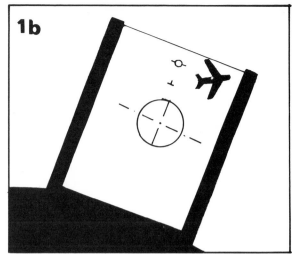

1b

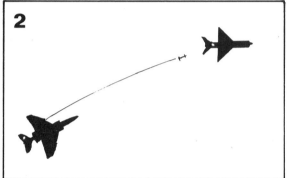

2

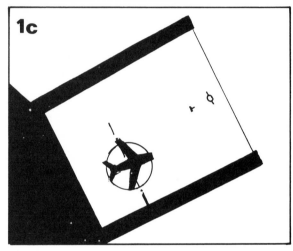

1c

3

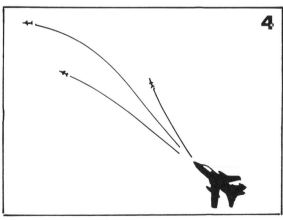

4

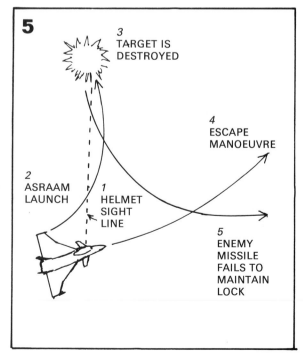

5

3 TARGET IS DESTROYED

4 ESCAPE MANOEUVRE

2 ASRAAM LAUNCH

1 HELMET SIGHT LINE

5 ENEMY MISSILE FAILS TO MAINTAIN LOCK

their lighter wing loadings; others have lower stalling speeds; some are best at high altitudes, others low down; some can make good use of a zoom climb, others cannot. The good fighter pilot will know the good and bad points of his own and of his opponent's performance envelope, and will be able to exploit these to the full. Although in air combat it is a well-known statistic that most kills are scored on the first pass, many battles *can* turn into a personalized duel between two opponents, and it is for these situations that the 'classic' dogfighting tactics are studied and practised.

Classic Dogfighting Techniques

The High-Speed Yo-Yo might be used where an opponent crosses in front of you, then turns towards you to prevent you getting on his tail. You pull up into a stalled turn to lose speed, then roll out into a dive behind your opponent.

The Low-Speed Yo-Yo would be used by the pursuing aircraft to break the stalemate of a turning dogfight where both aircraft are pulling close to the stall. The pursuer drops his nose to gain speed and rolls, so that when he pulls up again he will be closer to his quarry's Six o'Clock.

The Lag Pursuit Roll is used by a pursuing aircraft which has a speed advantage over its quarry. It uses this to chase it round the turn *on the outside*. In this position the quarry cannot see the pursuer, which aims to use its speed to get into the quarry's lethal cone. The transfer from the outside of the turn to the outside is accomplished by the pursuer doing a barrel roll across the track of the quarry.

Defensive manoeuvres are those which enable the quarry to turn the tables and become the pursuer. The best known of these is the *High-G Barrel Roll* which is used against a

121 The evolution of air combat techniques. (1a) – (1c) 1950s style; (a) the 'bounce'; (b) target breaks right; (c) gunsight pipper slews to allow attacking aircraft to aim ahead of the target.
(2) 1960s pursuit-course attack with early-model Sidewinder.
(3) 1980 beam attack with latest Sidewinder AIM-9L
(4) 1986 head-on engagement of multiple targets using BVR radar-guided missiles (AMRAAMs)
(5) 1990s-style engagement using ASRAAM, with helmet-pointing and lock-on after launch.

pursuer who is overtaking fast. Careful timing is needed if the quarry is to effect this manoeuvre to advantage. He throttles back and slams on the airbrakes before throwing his aircraft into a barrel roll which will leave him behind his opponent. A Harrier would use its famous 'viffing' ability to achieve the same result (VIFF = Vectoring in Forward Flight), slamming into vertical thrust while its pursuer passes underneath.

An aircraft which has a lower stalling speed than an opponent can use this to advantage, flying increasingly slowly in order to get behind an opponent. If both try to play this game the result is the deadly aerial ballet called *The Scissors* where the aircraft fly slowly round each other trying to position themselves for a shot. The first aircraft to break away, or the aircraft with the higher stalling speed, will prove the loser. *The Vertical Scissors* is played out in a downwards direction – the ultimate version of the game of Chicken.

However romantic the idea might sound, one-against-one dogfighting duels are not to be recommended. Two aircraft equally matched for performance, battling it out turn for turn in a fight to the death, with all their concentration directed to the task in hand, are easy prey to any other fighters who wish to intervene. Never fight alone – the day of the lone ace went out with Snoopy and the Red Baron. Fighters regularly fly as a defensive pair, or as it is sometimes called, a 'loose deuce', with about a mile of sky separating them, leader and wingman, each watching a different part of the sky and covering each other's Six o'Clock. The pair train together and develop a mutual understanding and almost total reliance upon each other. Complex tactics have been worked out for fighting in pairs and even more complex tactics for fighting in 'pairs of pairs'. Other tactical refinements cover the situations where approaching targets cannot easily be identified, where missiles of different kinds are likely to be used, or where the aircraft performances are widely dissimilar.

Dissimilar Combat Training

Following US experience in Vietnam, where F-4 Phantom pilots were surprised to find themselves outmanoeuvred by more lightly loaded

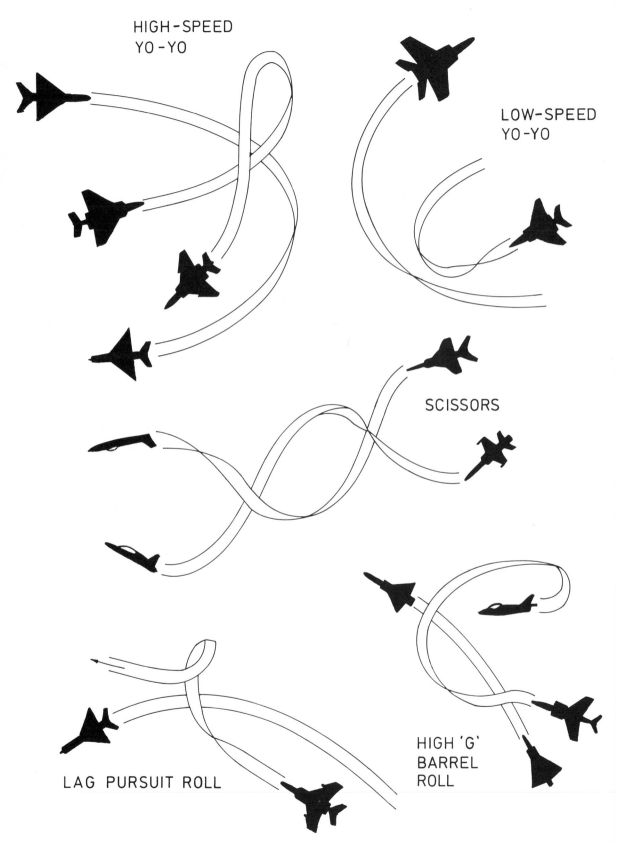

HIGH-SPEED
YO-YO

LOW-SPEED
YO-YO

SCISSORS

LAG PURSUIT ROLL

HIGH 'G'
BARREL
ROLL

123 Northrop F-5E Tiger II from a USAF 'aggressor' squadron, painted in simulated Warsaw Pact camouflage. (*Photograph courtesy USAF*)

124 An example of an F-16B, the two-seater conversion trainer, built for the Royal Netherlands Air Force and based at Leeuwarden. (*Photograph courtesy Koninklijke Luchtmacht*)

MiG-21s, the idea of 'dissimilar combat training' was introduced. Previous to this, Phantom pilots had only practised air combat against other Phantoms. Now combat pilots learn to 'fight' against a range of different types – Hawks, Phantoms, F-15s, F-16s, Mirages, Jaguars, F-5s, F-104s, Drakens, etc. – and, as one method of developing this idea, 'aggressor' squadrons have been instituted. A USAF aggressor squadron equipped with Northrop F-5E Tiger IIs is based at Alconbury in the UK and its role is to 'play the baddies' in giving USAFE and other allied pilots dissimilar combat training. The Alconbury F-5Es fly in simulated Warsaw Pact camouflage and their flying qualities are said to compare with those of the MiG-21 and -23.

Fighter pilots are notoriously tight-lipped when discussing combat tactics with outsiders. Israeli pilots do not give blow-by-blow accounts of how they outfought Syrian MiGs over the Bekaa Valley, and Royal Navy Sea Harrier pilots are loth to discuss whether or not they used their aircrafts' famous 'viffing' ability to advantage in the South Atlantic. Viffing is accomplished by slamming a Harrier's thrust nozzles into fast reverse in order to get behind an opponent quickly. At the time of the conflict, the media talked about little else, which may have led Argentine pilots to expect that they would be 'viffed'. Perhaps the Sea Harriers were just trying to gain a psychological advantage, but their success against them certainly was impressive. Good tactical training, teamwork, the latest Sidewinders and the amazing unreheated power of the Pegasus engine all contributed to earn the Sea Harrier its spurs as a dogfighter.

Air Combat Manoeuvring Instrumentation (ACMI)

One of the latest aids to training for complex combat is an electronic system known as Air Combat Manoeuvring Instrumentation (ACMI). This has been perfected by the US Navy and Air Force and the best known example has been installed at the NATO weapons training range at Decimomannu off the coast of Sardinia. Essen-

125 A side-by-side two-seat Lightning T.5 of the Lightning Training Flight prepares for take-off on a winter's day at Binbrook. (*Photograph courtesy RAF*)

tially, ACMI is a means of recording all the moves made during a simulated air combat and replaying and analyzing these on video afterwards. Aircraft taking part in the exercise carry a specially devised AIS (Airborne Instrumentation System) pod on one of their missile pylons. This pod is about the same size and weight as a Sidewinder and transmits flight data back to ground tracking stations for relaying to the system's computer. After the pilots have landed and are being debriefed, a video replay of the dogfight is available. The computer can be keyed to show the changing situation at any instant from any angle. This kind of aid is invaluable in providing training for complex fights where, above all else, *teamwork* has to be learned and practised.

THE OPERATIONAL CONVERSION UNIT (OCU)

Meanwhile, the student fast-jet pilots pass on from the Tactical Weapons Units to join an Operational Conversion Unit (OCU) where they will learn to fly the squadron aircraft to which they have been assigned. At the OCUs, they begin to fine-tune the tactical skills appropriate to their aircraft and its mission. Jaguar, Harrier, Tornado and Buccaneer pilots have to concentrate on getting through to their targets with their aircraft heavily laden with bombs, extra fuel, countermeasure pods, etc. They must fly low and aim to keep out of trouble, dodging round known defences where possible, or at the very least, running the gauntlet of these defences in a fast crossing pass where they will present the most difficult targets. Where several aircraft are assigned to the same target they will converge on it from different directions and, if they need to make several passes, they will fly a horizontal figure of eight, attacking each time from a different direction. Air combat pilots will begin to study and apply their own aircraft's tactical strengths, conceal its weaknesses, and make the most of its weapons system.

The OCUs have available a number of training aids such as two-seat aircraft and simulators. Transforming what was originally a single seat fighter into a two-seat, type-conversion trainer is not always easy, and the manufacturers have sometimes had to exercise some ingenuity in squeezing in the extra seat. In most types there is a tandem arrangement, one exception being the RAF's Lightning T.5 which has side-by-side seating.

Simulators have a number of advantages; they do not burn tons of expensive fuel and they cannot be damaged in crashes, so they represent a good training investment. The more elaborate simulators feel and handle just like the real thing and use elaborate computer-generated visual displays to complete the illusion of landing and taking off. The less elaborate simulators lack visual displays but they still constitute accurate replicas of the cockpit and aircraft systems and are invaluable for teaching emergency procedures. All manner of potentially dangerous airborne gremlins can be simulated – engine surges, bird strikes, hydraulic failures – without the simulator ever having to leave the ground. Other simulators can be used to train pilots in combat tactics or, what is perhaps more important, they can be programmed to investigate new tactical situations and to predict the best ways of responding to them.

Training never finishes. During peacetime a squadron pilot is undergoing training all the time and perfecting his flying and fighting skills: low flying, emergency procedures, cross-country flying, combat training, survival training, joint exercises and readiness evaluations such as TACEVAL. No amount of effort is spared to make these exercises as realistic as possible. Until recently, Tornado crews could only practise their low-flying skills in daylight, for fear of accidents. This precaution meant their pilots had little opportunity to use the Tornado's excellent automatic terrain-following abilities, and there was a fear that if the crews ever had to fly at low level at night or in bad weather they would feel at a disadvantage. As a result, and all-weather low-level training route through a thinly populated area of northern Scotland has been opened up and is in use from late afternoon until late evening.

NATO ALLIANCE JOINT EXERCISES

The NATO Alliance joint exercises reflect the truism that those who may have to fight together must train together. There is much coming and going between NATO air bases, and RAF pilots,

126 SK37 trainer version of the Saab Viggen, with extra cockpit 'grafted' on. (*Photograph courtesy Saab Scania*)

127 MiG-23U two-seat conversion trainers. (*Photograph courtesy Fotokhronika Tass*)

128 Two-seat conversion trainer McDonnell-Douglas F/A-18 Hornet. This example, plus the wing of the F-4 in the foreground, exemplifies the low-visibility camouflage and marking schemes now favoured by Allied air forces. (*Photograph courtesy McDonnell-Douglas*)

for example, become used to using German airfields and being vectored to their practice targets by Dutch fighter controllers. Some exercises are hosted by a particular nation, such as the annual Red Flag exercises held at Nellis Air Force Base near Las Vegas, Arizona, or the Maple Flag exercises held by the Canadian Forces at Cold Lake, Alberta. In the USA and Canada, unlike the UK or northern Europe, vast tracts of land and huge blocks of airspace are used for realistic air warfare 'games', with both air combat and ground-attack exercises.

Four NATO nations – the USA, the UK, Germany and Italy – share the running of the Decimomannu weapons range near Cape Frasca on Sardinia. The capabilities of the range have now been upgraded by the addition of an ACMI combat classroom.

In the UK there are severe restrictions on low-level flying and, apart from weapons-training ranges, no special areas have been designated for low-level flying. At high-level, however, things are different and the upper airspace above North Wales, north Yorkshire, Lincolnshire and parts of the West Country has been designated as Military Training Airspace. The blocks of sky in question extend from an altitude of 24,500ft (about 7470m) up to 45,000ft (about 13,700m). On a clear day the contorted vapour trails can be seen criss-crossing the sky and it goes without saying that civil air traffic is rarely, if ever, routed through these areas.

Much has been written and said about the future of military aviation and, in particular, about air combat. It was all being said 30 years ago at the dawn of the air-to-air missile era, and now the armchair strategists are saying it again: dogfighting is out. According to them, the future must certainly lie with improved medium- and long-range missiles for head-on engagements BVR, and, for short-range fighting, on very manoeuvrable missiles which can acquire their targets by helmet-pointing or by locking-on after launch. Do we really need new, agile fighters, when what we surely need is more ECM-resistant radars and missiles and improved methods of target identification at long range? The armchair strategists have been proved wrong before. Why should they be right this time?

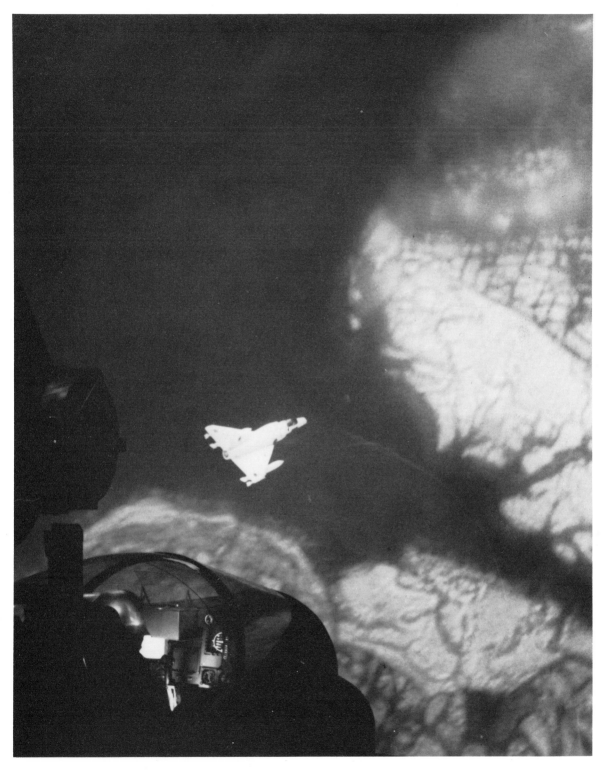

129 Visual display from BAe Warton's twin-dome air-
combat simulator. (*Photograph courtesy British Aerospace*)

130 Saab 105 trainer and light strike fighter of the Austrian Air Force. (*Photograph courtesy Bundesministerium für Landesverteidigung*)

131 Boeing T-43 navigational trainer. (*Photograph courtesy Boeing*)

8 *Other Roles*

Refuelling tactical aircraft in flight, providing logistical support, providing tactical support by landing or dropping troops and equipment, evacuating casualties, airlifting personnel, transporting VIPs – including heads of state and government ministers – ferrying spares and fuel, maritime patrol, search and rescue, mountain rescue, firefighting, disaster relief, weather and ice patrolling, calibrating navigational aids and performing at flying displays are all tasks that military aircraft, both fixed-wing and helicopters, perform either routinely or are called upon to perform at some time or another. Many of these 'utility' roles keep entire squadrons far busier and flying many more hours per week than their tactical squadron counterparts in normal peacetime.

FLIGHT REFUELLING

On the night of 30 April/1May 1982 RAF Vulcan B.2 XM607 flew the longest bombing raid in history from Ascension Island to Port Stanley and back. Twenty-one 1000lb (454kg) bombs were dropped, only one of which hit the airfield runway, but this was enough to make it unusable by the Argentinian Mirages and Skyhawks. To deliver this one bomb the Vulcan had to be refuelled in flight four times on the way out and four times on the way back by Victor K.2 tankers. Some of the Victors themselves had to be refuelled in flight, and, allowing for spare tankers and emergency arrangements, a total of 13 Victors took off from Ascension Island to get this one bomb on the runway.

In-flight refuelling of tactical aircraft extends their range and keeps their vulnerable airfields well back out of a possible enemy's reach. It would be central to any full-scale use of air power at the present day. In the air defence of the United Kingdom Phantoms and Tornado F.2s would be refuelled in flight in order to extend their combat radius and combat air-patrol endurance.

The RAF's flight refuelling system uses the probe-and-drogue technique which is also favoured by the US Navy. The USAF uses the rather different boom-and-slipway system. Although the two systems are incompatible in their basic form, each has advantages, and the French Air Force had been able to devise a hybrid technique.

With the probe-and-drogue system, the tanker aircraft trails a basket-shaped drogue. The receiving aircraft is fitted with a forward-facing probe, fixed in the case of some aircraft such as the Buccaneer, retractable in the case of most others such as the Phantom and Tornado. The pilot of the receiving aircraft has to fly his probe into the basket of the drogue, where it locks and fuel begins to flow.

The US Air Force KC-135 flying tankers are equipped with the Boeing-designed flying boom which is 'piloted' by a crewman lying prone at a window underneath the tail. The receiver aircraft takes up its station behind and below the tanker while the boom operator guides the boom extension into a slipway door somewhere on the receiver's upper fuselage. Connection is made and fuel starts to flow. This system is ideal for refuelling large aircraft because it can deliver fuel more quickly than by means of probe-and-drogue, but it has the disadvantage that it needs an operator located in the tanker aircraft's tail. This would be difficult to arrange in the case of a small carrier-borne aircraft such as the US Navy's KS-3A Viking tanker. Space is also at a premium aboard the RAF's Victors, so the passive trailing of a drogue is preferred to the complications of the flying boom. The French use KC-135 tankers, but they fit a drogue to the end of the boom

132   A Tornado is refuelled from a Victor K.2 tanker. (*Photograph courtesy British Aerospace*)

133   Probe and drogue refuelling in close-up. The retractable probe of a Phantom plugged into the drogue being trailed by a Victor tanker. The lights around the drogue basket are for use at night. (*Photograph courtesy RAF*)

134   Flight refuelling probe fitted to a Nimrod MR.2

135   Boom-and-slipway refuelling seen from the operator's station aboard a US Air Force KC-135 tanker. The A-10 Thunderbolt II is receiving fuel via a trapdoor in the nose. (*Photograph courtesy John Downey*)

when they require to refuel probe-equipped fighters.

The RAF's Victors are to be supplemented by a mixed tanker fleet of converted VC-10 and Tristar airliners, ex-British Airways. Meanwhile the US Air Force has ordered a fleet of McDonnell-Douglas KC-10A Extenders advanced tanker/cargo aircraft, based on the DC-10 airliner. The Extenders and Tristars will be able to carry passengers and cargo as well as fuel for in-flight refuelling and their main purpose is to help with the rapid deployment of whole squadrons of fighters to wherever they are needed, by carrying the squadron's equipment and personnel while refuelling the fighters in mid-air.

During in-flight refuelling it may be difficult to match the speeds of both tanker and receiver aircraft. On RAF flights between Ascension Island and the Falklands, a Hercules can only keep station with a VC-10 while being refuelled if both aircraft fly downhill in a shallow dive. For its part a Herk is about the only aircraft which can fly slowly enough to refuel a helicopter.

136   Study of a Victor K.2 tanker

137   A Lockheed C-130 Hercules is one of the few aircraft which can fly slowly enough to refuel a helicopter, in this case a Sikorsky CH-3 Jolly Green Giant. (*Photograph courtesy Lockheed Georgia Company*)

TRANSPORT

The Lockheed C-130 Hercules has seen service in so many different places carrying out such a wide-variety of different jobs that whole books have been written about this plane alone. It is easily the most widely used tactical and utility transport since the Dakota, serving with the air and naval forces of 55 nations and with a few airlines as a cargo carrier. The Herk first flew in 1954 and its most innovative feature was the rear ramp, which can be lowered in flight to drop supplies, paratroops, equipment, sonobuoys and ordnance. In the South Atlantic in 1982 the Argentine Air Force even tried to use the C-130 as a bomber to attack ships supplying the British Task Force. In its primary role of tactical transport, the Hercules has to be capable of flying low when necessary to avoid enemy defences, and of landing and taking off from short roughly prepared runways. The main hold is unpressurized, but there is provision to pressurize the crew compartment if required.

The RAF ordered 66 C-130H Herks and, with the sale of the Belfasts some years ago, it found itself short of carrying capacity. One solution has been to 'stretch' 30 of their Herks to Super Hercules (Lockheed C-100-30) standard. The

138   The ubiquitous multi-role Hercules in the colours of the Royal Danish Air Force. (*Photograph courtesy Flyveaabnet*)

139   In need of extra carrying capacity, the RAF has had several of its Hercules fleet 'stretched' to Super Hercules dimensions as in this example. (*Photograph courtesy RAF*)

140 Santa Claus Act – A Hercules demonstrates one of its tricks – LAPES (Low Altitude Parachute Extraction System). (*Photograph courtesy Lockheed Georgia Company*)

work has been carried out mostly by Marshalls of Cambridge who also fitted flight-refuelling probes to some of the fleet at the time of the South Atlantic crisis. Since then, RAF Herks have been able to fly to Stanley, where they also function in AEW and flight-refuelling roles.

The Armée de l'Air operates the Noratlas and the C-160 Transall as tactical transports and, because of a continuing demand for Transalls, the production line was recently restarted. The Transall is assembled by Aerospatiale and powered by two Rolls-Royce Tyne turboprops, giving it a MTOW of about three-quarters that of the Hercules.

Other tactical transports are the Aeritalia G.222, the Antonov An-12 and An-22, the De Havilland Canada DHC-4 Caribou and DHC-5 Buffalo and the Lockheed C-141 Starlifter and C-5 Galaxy. Of these, the huge Galaxy is by far the biggest, weighing 169 tonnes empty, and 349 tonnes all-up, of which 100 tonnes would be payload. Only the Galaxy is capable of airlifting two M-1 battle tanks, and to make loading and unloading easier it can, like the Transall, semi-retract its multi-wheel main undercarriage into a 'kneeling' position. Recently, the USSR has unveiled its own Galaxy look-alike, the even larger Antonov An-400 transport, codenamed 'Condor'.

Civilians in Warpaint

Besides these tactical transports, almost every airliner, cargo plane or biz-jet which has ever done duty plying the civil air routes of the world has donned warpaint and been pressed into military service at some stage or other of its career. Examples are too numerous to give a mention to all, but here are a few. The McDonnell-Douglas DC-9-30 airliner serves with the USAF as a flying hospital, rechristened C-9 Nightingale. The British Aerospace 748 serves with the RAF as the Andover transport, while one or two are operated by 115 Squadron to check and calibrate radio navigation aids. (Meanwhile, the manufacturers are offering the multi-role 748 mainly for inshore maritime reconnaissance.) The odd-looking, Belfast-built Shorts Skyvan serves as a utility transport with the Sultan of Oman's Air Force, while its larger brother, the Shorts Sherpa has been ordered for the US Air Force. Sleek, luxury airliners, such as the Fokker F-28 Fellowship and business jets, such as the B.Ae125, have been chosen for transporting cabinet ministers and heads of state about their business. In Britain, we have 32 Squadron based at RAF Northolt, the nearest airfield to the centre of London and equipped with B.Ae125-700s, Andovers and a selection of helicopters.

Sometimes, though, the process is reversed. Military aircraft are demobilized to achieve fame in civilian life. The Boeing 367-80 was designed to a military specification and

141 Boeing Vertol CH-47 Chinook twin rotor heavylift helicopters of No. 18 Squadron, based at RAF Odiham. The Chinooks are seen here taxi-ing in their characteristic nose-up 'praying mantis' attitude. (*Photograph courtesy RAF, British Crown Copyright reserved*)

spawned the C-135 (transport), KC-135 (tanker), RC-135 (reconnaissance) and EC-135 (electronic intelligence), but we know the design best as the familiar Boeing 707 airliner. More recently the Brazilian Government wanted its native aerospace industry to produce a range of small, utility military planes. The result was the C-95 transport, the EC-95 for electronic calibration the RC-95 for reconnaissance, the P-95 for maritime patrol, and of course, the Embraer Bandeirante commuterliner.

Utility Helicopters

The specialized assault helicopter with its flat plate windshields, low frontal area and racks of rockets and missiles aimed at their targets by cunning electro-optical devices has been described already. The one helicopter which most endeared itself to troops in Vietnam was the Bell UH-1 'Huey', unarmed except for the door gunners, which could ferry troops to forward areas, keep them covered as they disembarked and advanced, then if necessary evacuate any casualties. Over terrain which is too difficult for wheeled vehicles and even for tanks, such as Northern Norway or the Falklands, helicopters will have to take on the main burden of ferrying troops, supplies, ammunition and equipment, and this is where the ability of some choppers to pick up heavy loads becomes crucial. The

142 Inshore maritime patrol. A Fokker F-27 Maritime of the Koninklijke Luchtmacht in service in the Netherlands Antilles. (*Photograph courtesy Fokker*)

Chinook is the RAF's heavylift helicopter, followed closely by the Sea King and the Puma, but the mightiest helo of them all is the Soviet Union's Mi-26 Halo which is as big as an airliner and capable of carrying up to 90 fully equipped troops.

FIREFIGHTERS

Aircraft can be used to fight fires which they dowse with water or flame-retardant chemicals. Once again, the Hercules has been used, but the most interesting fire-fighter is the Canadair CL-215 water bomber. This can carry about 1210 gallons (over 5500 litres) of water which it discharges in one second over a forest fire. The CL-215 refills its water tanks by landing on a lake and taxi-ing while it scoops up another load of water. These water-bombers are operated by France, Spain, Greece, and Yugoslavia to quench the dangerous brush fires which are liable to erupt during the dry summer months around the Mediterranean shores.

INSHORE MARITIME PATROL

A maritime nation enjoys exclusive economic rights to its offshore waters extending out to 200 nautical miles from its coasts, and those rights include fishing, minerals and oil. These are valuable assets which must be safeguarded from illegal fishing, pollution or interference. Problems can also arise through attempts at illegal immigration or the smuggling of drugs and arms, and there is an ever-present call on Search and Rescue services. Nations which operate ASW aircraft such as Nimrods, Orions or Atlantiques can use them for inshore maritime patrol. It may seem ridiculous to chase illegal fishing boats in an aircraft the size of a Nimrod, but if the Nimrods and their crews are available anyway, equipped and trained for inshore as well as ASW duties, why not use them?

At both St. Mawgan and Kinloss there is always a Nimrod and its crew available on SAR standby. If scrambled they can be airborne quickly and, proceeding at high speed to the emergency, they use their powerful radar, radio-homing equipment, searchlight and the eyes of every spare member of the crew to comb thousands of square miles of ocean in a

143 Turbine-powered Islander operated on behalf of the UK Ministry of Agriculture Fisheries and Food

methodical fashion. If anything is located, a Nimrod cannot land to render assistance, but it can summon help from helicopters or surface craft and, if necessary, drop flares, smoke markers, liferafts or medical equipment. On occasion, doctors and even bomb-disposal experts have been known to jump out of Nimrods and parachute into the sea. For dropping smoke markers, the Nimrod possesses an ingenious ejector which propels the flare backwards at the same speed as the aircraft is moving forwards, causing it to fall straightdown into the sea. Some countries operate floatplanes or amphibians in the SAR role, such as the Japanese Shin Meiwa PS-1 or the Soviets' Beriev Be-12 Tchaika, but these are less useful than they seem because they cannot land or take off in very rough seas. In such conditions they too have to leave the difficult operations to the helicopters and surface craft. Around the shores of the UK, a number of both RAF and Royal Navy helicopters are available for maritime SAR and for cliff or mountain rescue.

Several hundred Operation Tapestry Nimrod flights are requested and paid for by the UK Ministry of Agriculture, Fisheries and Food, which also operates a number of smaller civil aircraft in its own right, such as the Pilatus Britten Norman Islander. Although all EEC fishing waters are shared, the UK is responsible for looking after what is by far the largest area and for ensuring that fishery laws are being complied with. It might seem unlikely that a high-performance aircraft flashing past at 250 knots (288mph) at 200ft (60m) would be able to tell which variety of fish are being caught, but Nimrods are very successful at bringing prosecutions for illegal fishing. Flying at 200ft (60m) there is a 20 mile (32km) radar horizon, and the visual horizon is about the same distance away. Every craft shows on radar and it is not possible for a fishing boat to haul in her nets before the Nimrod is there to check her registered number and take a photograph. If something is amiss, the Nimrod will go round again and take more photographs, and these will show an Omega navigational fix – evidence enough to convict the culprit in any EEC court of law and inflict severe penalties. The oil and gas rigs in the North Sea and the Celtic Sea are also patrolled by Nimrods on Operation Tapestry flights.

An air force or navy requiring something just a bit smaller than a Nimrod for inshore maritime

144   Learjet 35A used by the Finnish Air Force for a variety of patrol, reconnaissance and general duties, including target-towing. (*Photograph courtesy Ilmavoimat*)

145   Belfast-built Short Skyvan of the Sultan of Oman's Air Force. (*Photograph courtesy Shorts*)

146   Bell UH-1 Iroquois helicopters ('Hueys' to their friends) in action for real, providing cover for advancing troops in Vietnam. Note the door gunners. (*Photograph courtesy Bell Helicopters*)

patrolling would probably choose an adaptation of a well-proven transport or utility aircraft. The version would need to be specially built from the word go, with extra corrosion-protection – absolutely essential for flying so close to the the sea – built in at all stages. Possibilities include the B.Ae Multi-Role Coastguarder, the Fokker F-27 Maritime, the Dassault Breguet Gardian, the GAF Searchmaster, or maritime versions of the Hercules or Transall.

A different philosophy – that of high-altitude maritime reconnaissance – is sometimes adopted. The Indonesian Air Force operates a number of Boeing 737s in the maritime-reconnaissance role. These are equipped with dorsal-mounted Motorola SLAMMR (Side-looking Advanced Multimode Maritime Radar) which,

from high altitude, can map a swath of ocean out to 100 nautical miles either side. Anything suspicious detected by the radar is passed to helicopters or surface craft for further investigation. The speed and altitude at which the 737 can operate mean that it can check a large area of ocean quickly and economically.

Sideways-looking radar installations provide high-resolution imagery which is sharp enough even to detect oil pollution at sea. The Swedish Coast Guard has used the idea for some years, carrying lightweight SLAR aboard Cessna 337s. Oil slicks produce flatter waves which show up as characteristic patches on the radar display. The UK Department of Transport has now installed similar equipment aboard civil-chartered Islanders.

147 More live action. An Aerospatiale Alouette operated by the Gendarmerie rescues an injured climber in the French Pyrenees.

149 Members of the crew of a Tu-16 of soviet Naval Aviation. (*Photograph courtesy RAF*)

148 Westland Commando helicopter used by Egypt for VIP transport duties. (*Photograph courtesy Westland*)

9 Observing Military Aircraft

The best opportunity that most people have to observe military aircraft is provided by the air shows and flying displays which take place mainly in the summer months. These events are organized by the industry, as in the case of Farnborough, by a charity, as in the case of Greenham Common, by the manufacturers, or by the Services. They are well advertized both locally and in the aviation press and, in the case of airfields in holiday areas – such as RAF Valley, RAF Brawdy, RAF St Mawgan, RNAS Yeovilton and RNAS Culdrose – the Open Days are held during the holiday months of July and August. These events provide the organizers with a very good piece of public relations, while the aviation enthusiasts and members of the public who attend have the opportunity to observe and photograph many current types of military aircraft in the air and on the ground.

If you like photography you can get quite good results with a simple camera, but the serious aviation photographer equips himself with a 35mm outfit, preferably a single lens reflex with interchangeable lenses. The standard 50mm lens (which has an equivalent field of view to the lens on a simple camera) should be suitable for general scenes, some of the exhibits in the static park – including detail close-ups – and *formation* flying scenes such as those provided by the Red Arrows. For long-range shots, long-range detail, and flying displays featuring single aircraft, you will need the help of a telephoto lens (around 200mm) or a zoom lens. Load with fast film.

At an air show, *people* can be quite a nuisance. There in the static park is what you have come hundreds of miles to see – some of the rarest military aircraft in the Western hemisphere, each one surrounded by hordes of human admirers crowding right up to the barrier. By the time you have managed to squeeze your way to the front of the throng, you are nose-up against the radome – so close to the plane that you cannot get a photograph unless you use a wide angle lens.

There are other crowd-defeating measures you can adopt. Try arriving really early in the day and queueing so as to be one of the first inside as soon as the gates open. It also helps to arrive on foot, not trying to bring your car right in. If you didn't manage to get there early, try staying late after most of the crowds have left and are sitting in traffic jams. You should then have the aircraft (and mountains of litter) almost to yourself, until somebody arrives to tell you that the gates are closing in five minutes.

The biennial military aircraft tattoo at Greenham Common has grown to become the biggest and best show of its kind in Europe, and has a number of unique features. There are often visits from some of the rarest species, such as the SR-71 Blackbird. The always-exciting Red Arrows are joined by corresponding formation aerobatic teams from abroad, such as the Patrouille de France in their Alpha Jets, Il Frecce Tricolori with MB.339s, the Austrian Karo As in their Saab 105s and the F-16s of the USAF Thunderbirds. Helicopter display teams also abound, such as the Royal Navy's exciting Sharks in their Gazelles from Culdrose. With the help of the open-topped 'photobuses' laid on by the Greenham organizers, it is possible to tour the aircraft in the static displays and take excellent photographs without the need for special close-up lenses. Another feature is that the airfield is open to aviation enthusiasts for the two days before and one day after the main flying display weekend, providing relatively crowd-free opportunities to watch arrivals and departures or to take photographs in the static

150 The Sharks formation helicopter display team (Westland Gazelles) from No. 715 Naval Air Squadron, RNAS Culdrose. (*Photograph courtesy Royal Navy*)

park, but to gain admittance on these additional days it is necessary to join the FIAT (Friends of the Air Tattoo) organization. For details of membership charges and other information, write to: FIAT, Building 91, RAF Greenham Common, Newbury, Berks, RG15 8HL. The 1985 Air Tattoo will be held at RAF Fairford.

The Farnborough Air Show, which takes place biennially in early September, is unique in other ways. Besides military types, civil aircraft are also represented and, because Farnborough is a trade fair for the entire aerospace industry, missiles, avionics and weapons systems are on display in the static park and much useful information can be gleaned by visiting the exhibition halls.

Don't forget that the past is the key to the present and that there is much to be learned, even about present-day aircraft, from visiting aviation museums; the RAF Museum at Hendon, the Imperial War Museum at Lambeth, with its annexe at Duxford just off the M11 in Cambridgeshire, the Fleet Air Arm Museum at Yeovilton, the Manchester Air and Space Museum, and so on. Every little helps in an effort to build up an understanding of today's military aircraft and how they work. Periodicals such as *Flight International*, *Air Pictorial*, etc. make interesting reading, and you can often meet people who can loan you entire sets of back numbers.

Another good idea is to join an aviation

151 Mil Mi-2 helicopters take part in a display to celebrate USSR Air Force Day, August 15 1982. (*Photograph courtesy Fotokhronika Tass*)

society. Although many of these are locally based, they often have a nationwide membership through their specialist publications – for example, the Merseyside Aviation Society, c/o Liverpool Airport, or the West London Aviation Group. Besides providing useful information to members through their publications, these societies hold regular meetings with guest speakers on all aspects of civil and military aviation, and they can sometimes arrange visits to military airfields or cheap travel to events such as the Paris Salon Air Show at Le Bourget.

Military airfields are scattered throughout Britain, by far the biggest concentration being in East Anglia. Unless you visit these bases on Open Days or by special arrangement through an aviation society, the chances are that you can only observe their activities through the chain-link perimeter fence. Plane-spotting is a popular British pastime and the authorities are usually tolerant of spectators who approach these bases armed with cameras and binoculars, *provided they stay outside the fence*. The approach end of the runway is by far the most popular location and, even without special equipment, it is possible to take quite good photographs of aircraft coming in to land. Crash gates are also convenient vantage points.

Although some bases are active at weekends, most flying at UK military airfields takes place Monday to Friday. Normally you need to be free during the week to make the most of military plane-spotting possibilities. Opportunities can arise when you are on holiday, even out-of-season, and some British holiday areas, such as the West Country, West Wales, East Yorkshire and East Anglia, are well-supplied with airfields within easy reach. To locate the best vantage points around your chosen airfield, it pays to refer to an Ordnance Survey map. But don't trespass on private farmland.

Although there may be no restriction in the UK on observing or photographing aircraft from outside the fence of a military airfield, don't assume that these freedoms necessarily apply in other countries, particularly in Eastern Europe. Many an aviation enthusiast or photographer has got himself into serious trouble when pursuing his interest abroad. The hospitality of the local jail is not to be preferred to that of your hotel, so be warned!

Watching out for military overflights is good fun and quite rewarding. Not all of the vapour trails which criss-cross the blue sky on a clear

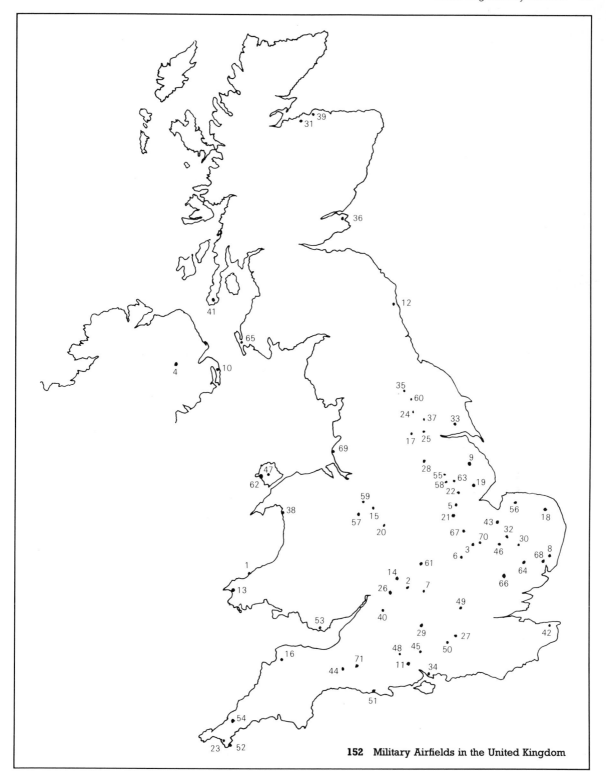

152 **Military Airfields in the United Kingdom**

Military Airfields in the United Kingdom

No.	Airfield	TACAN	Main Unit(s) Based	Aircraft Types
1	Aberporth	—	MOD (PE)	—
2	Abingdon	—	UAS, AEF, MU	Bulldog, Chipmunk, Jaguar
3	Alconbury	ALC	USAF 10 TRW	RF-4, F-5, TR-1
4	Aldergrove	AGV	72 Sqn	Wessex
5	Barkston Heath	—	R (*see Cranwell*)	—
6	Bedford	—	MOD (PE)	—
7	Benson	—	115 Sqn	Andover
8	Bentwaters	BTW	USAF 81 TFW	A-10
9	Binbrook	BNK	5, 11 Sqns	Lightning
10	Bishops Court	—	RAF	—
11	Boscombe Down	BDH	MOD (PE)	—
12	Boulmer	—	202 Sqn SAR	Sea King
13	Brawdy	BDY	TWU, 202 Sqn	Hawk, Sea King HAR.3
14	Brize Norton	BZN	10, 216 Sqn	VC-10 Tristar
15	Chetwynd	—	R (*see Shawbury*)	—
16	Chivenor	CVR	TWU, 22 Sqn	Hawk, Wessex
17	Church Fenton	—	7 FTS	Jet Provost
18	Coltishall	CSL	6, 41, 54, 22 Sqn.	Jaguar, Wessex
19	Coningsby	CGY	29 Sqn	Tornado F.2
20	Cosford	—	UAS, AEF	Bulldog, Chipmunk
21	Cottesmore	CTM	TTTE	Tornado
22	Cranwell	—	RAF College	Jet Provost
23	Culdrose	—	Royal Navy	Sea King, Gazelle, Jetstream
24	Dishforth	—	R (*see Leeming*)	—
25	Elvington	—	R (*see Linton-on-Ouse*)	—
26	Fairford	FFA	USAF	KC-135
27	Farnborough	—	MOD (PE)	—
28	Finningley	—	6 FTS, UAS, AEF	Jet Provost, Dominie, Jetstream
29	Greenham Common	GCN	USAF	—
30	Honington	—	9, 208, Sqn TWCU	Tornado GR.1 Buccaneer
31	Kinloss	KSS	120, 201, 206 Sqn	Nimrod MR.2
32	Lakenheath	LKH	USAF 48 TFW	F-111F
33	Leconfield	—	22 Sqn	Wessex
34	Lee-on-Solent	—	Royal Navy	Naval helicopters
35	Leeming	—	UAS, AEF	Bulldog, Jet Provost, Tornado F.2
36	Leuchars	LUK	43, 111, 22 Sqn	Phantom, Wessex, Tornado F.2
37	Linton-on-Ouse	—	1 FTS	Jet Provost
38	Llanbedr	—	MOD (PE)	—
39	Lossiemouth	—	12, 202 Sqns	Buccaneer
40	Lyneham	—	24, 30, 47, 70 Sqns	Hercules
41	Macrihanish	MAZ	RAF	—
42	Manston	—	22 Sqn, AEF	Wessex, Chipmunk
43	Marham	—	55, 67, 617 Sqns	Tornado, GR.1, VC-10.
44	Merryfield	—	R (*see Yeovilton*)	—
45	Middle Wallop	—	Army Air Corps	Lynx, Gazelle
46	Mildenhall	MLD	USAF 513 TAW	C-130, KC-135

Military Airfields in the United Kingdom*Continued*

No.	Airfield	TACAN	Main Unit(s) Based	Aircraft Types
47	Mona	—	R (*see Valley*)	—
48	Netheravon	—	Army Air Corps	Lynx
49	Northolt	—	32, 207 Sqns	HS.125, Devon
50	Odiham	ODH	7, 33, 18 Sqn	Chinook, Puma
51	Portland	—	Royal Navy	Naval helicopters
52	Predannack	—	R (*see Culdrose*)	—
53	St. Athan	—	UAS	Bulldog
54	St. Mawgan	SMG	42 Sqn.	Nimrod MR.2
55	Scampton	—	Red Arrows CFS.	Hawk, Jet Provost
56	Sculthorpe	SKT	USAF	—
57	Shawbury	—	2 FTS	Gazelle, Wessex, Jet Provost
58	Swinderby	—	FSS	Chipmunk
59	Ternhill	—	R (*see Shawbury*)	—
60	Topcliffe	—	R (*see Leeming*)	—
61	Upper Heyford	UPH	USAF 20 TFW	F-111E
62	Valley	VYL	2 FTS, 22 Sqn	Hawk, Wessex
63	Waddington	—	8 Sqn.	Nimrod AEW.3
64	Wattisham	WTM	43, 56, 111, 74, Sqns	Phantom F4J
65	West Freugh	—	MOD (PE)	—
66	Wethersfield	WET	USAF	—
67	Wittering	WIT	1 Sqn	Harrier GR.3
68	Woodbridge	WDB	USAF (*see Bentwaters*)	—
69	Woodvale	—	UAS, AEF	—
70	Wyton	—	1 PRU, 13, 360 Sqn	Canberra, Nimrod R.1
71	Yeovilton	VLN	Royal Navy	Sea Harrier, Wessex

Abbreviations

AEF	Air Experience Flight
FSS	Flying Selection Squadron
FTS	Flying Training School
MOD (PE)	Ministry of Defence Procurement Executive
PRU	Photographic Reconnaissance Unit
R	Relief landing ground
SAR	Search and Rescue
TAW	Tactical Airlift Wing
TFW	Tactical Fighter Wing
TRW	Tactical Reconnaissance Wing
TTTE	Tri-national Tornado Training Establishment
TWCU	Tornado Weapons Conversion Unit
TWU	Tactical Weapons Unit
UAS	University Air Squadrons

day are made by airliners plying their trade along the air routes and, with the help of a pair of binoculars, you can often pick out military types going about their high-flying business. Keep an eye out too, for low-level overflights. Many parts of Britain are used for low-level training, in fact those parts which are *not* overflown are the exception (for example, the zones of civil controlled airspace surrounding the major airports). Frequently during the week, when one is driving along a motorway such as the M5, or walking in the hills, a Phantom, Jaguar, Hawk, A-10, F-111 or Tornado will flash past. Helicopters, too, often make low-level cross-country flights. Keep your eyes and ears open; you never know what will turn up next.

153 Alpha Jets of the Patrouille de France aerobatic team. (*Photograph courtesy AMD-BA*)

154 A-10 at Farnborough displays a variety of sophisticated weaponry seldom seen in public elsewhere. A Pave Penny laser tracker is mounted close to the nosewheel leg, while the other pylons carry an assortment of weapons including a Maverick missile, a Paveway laser-guided bomb, a HOBOS TV-guided bomb, a clutch of 'iron' bombs, and on the extreme right, an AN/ALQ-119 ECM jammer pod.

Index